995

New
Orleans
⤜ in the ⤛
FORTIES

Hotel New Orleans and Joy Theater on Canal Street in the late forties.

New Orleans
≫ in the ≪
FORTIES

Mary Lou Widmer

Foreword by Frank Schneider

Pelican Publishing Company
GRETNA 1990

Library of Congress Cataloging-in-Publication Data

Widmer, Mary Lou, 1926-
    New Orleans in the forties / Mary Lou Widmer ; foreword by Frank
Schneider.
        p.   cm.
    Includes index.
    ISBN 0-88289-814-0
    1. New Orleans (La.)—Civilization.   2. New Orleans (La.)—
Description—Views.   I. Title.
F379.N55W54 1990
976.3'35—dc20   90-38100
                                                                CIP

Manufactured in the United States of America
Published by Pelican Publishing Company, Inc.
1101 Monroe Street, Gretna, Louisiana 70053

This book is dedicated to my lovely grown children and their wonderful spouses: Jay and Carla and Dana and Tommy.

The Jerusalem Temple was the scene of many high school proms and parties in the 1940s.

Contents

A peaceful stroll through Audubon Park in the forties.

Foreword

Is there anything sweeter than calling to mind moments of our past? Frequently, we do so as we remember them, rather than as they were. But with that aside, the degree to which we achieve our elusive goal known as happiness depends upon our ability to recall the joyful times. If you're having trouble with that, Mary Lou Widmer's book makes it easier.

New Orleans in the Forties jogs our thoughts and sets them on a proper course. Here are the facts—the nostalgic truth—about life in New Orleans in the forties. If by some chance we have been stricken by some strange malady and forgotten something memorable about the world as it was, the author's story sets down names, dates, places, song titles, historical facts, football scores—every detail—before us.

Remember the blitzkrieg, when Adolf Hitler goose-stepped across Europe . . . and Orleanians went on living as usual? Enter World War II. The miserable disaster that could not happen, did. Lives changed, directions were altered, plans were postponed. Orleanians lit candles and prayed for victory.

The young men were leaving, Rosie became a riveter, the fair sex motored the streetcars, sugar was rationed, Hitler died, Benito Mussolini died, Franklin Roosevelt died, Japan surrendered, war ended. But before that, Mary Lou Schultis was building memories: jitterbugging to Val Barbara's band on the steamer *President*, riding the trolleys for seven cents, buying jelly beans at Kress, reveling at LSU games, living it up in tulle with corsage at the Blue Room, and exclaiming "swell" to almost anything.

Just about everything that made the forties memorable is mentioned in this delightfully constructed book. The author uses information from newspaper ads and stories to chronicle the times that are meshed with accounts of her personal life—her teenage years with friend Audrey, her relationship with family, and how she deliberately set out to get her name changed to Widmer.

Younger readers may be astounded by—perhaps even doubt—the sweet innocence of their moms and dads who came up in another time not so very long ago. Those were the days when gentleness was spread around generously like free fertilizer that cultivated trust.

NEW ORLEANS
IN THE FORTIES

It was the late forties. Chep Morrison was mayor. Earl K. Long was governor. And Mary Lou Widmer's story ends. But the memories linger. Cherish them.

FRANK SCHNEIDER

Preface

OF ALL THE DECADES in the twentieth century, none is more difficult to re-create than the forties. During the four years of World War II, New Orleanians, like all Americans, vacillated between hope and despair. Although a half-century has passed, the war, with its atrocities and its toll of 50 million lives, still stands like a monolith, casting a long shadow over the succeeding decades.

Our World War II veterans will tell you that it was the high point of drama in their lives, and that nothing since has come anywhere near it for sheer excitement. It was a time of violence and virtue, of massacre and survival, of fear and exhilaration.

Our memories of the events leading up to the war, our losses and deprivations during the war, and our fears in its aftermath affected us profoundly. Those of us who lived through it could never possibly be quite the same again.

It was a decade of giants, good and evil. Some of them had entered the world arena in the thirties, but had not been pressed to reveal their full capacity for good or evil until the forties. Adolf Hitler, Winston Churchill, Joseph Stalin, and Franklin D. Roosevelt played the lead roles. Among the postwar leaders were Charles de Gaulle, the architect of modern France, and Marshal Tito, who ruled Yugoslavia until his death in 1980.

In New Orleans, where change happened slowly in the best of times, no physical changes occurred during the years 1942–45 because of a moratorium on civilian building due to a shortage of materials and labor. Streets became cracked and potholed. Houses and commercial buildings fell into disrepair.

The people of our city grieved for their lost sons or husbands; obeyed the air-raid instructions; suffered the shortages of sugar, meat, and gasoline in good spirits; and collected everything from metal to bacon grease for the war effort. We bought war bonds and paid a Victory Tax to help defray the astronomical expenses of guns and tanks and battleships. We wore our hair in Victory bobs, and grew Victory gardens in our backyards. We car-pooled or took public transit when our gasoline ration books were out of stamps. We had servicemen to Sunday dinner, hoping that families in distant cities were doing the same for our husbands and sweethearts and sons. At Mass, we prayed for victory and lit candles for the safe return of our loved ones.

In the defense plants on the lakefront and in the New Orleans area, women took jobs men would have done, to free men for combat. "Rosie the Riveter" became more than just a song. And in the civilian world, women became street-car conductors and linemen for the telephone company. They were entering the work force and would find that they liked it there. Never again would women as a whole stay home, keep house, and have babies.

More events of earth-shattering importance happened in 1945 than in any other year of the century, or perhaps in all of our history up to that time. Hitler died, Mussolini died, Roosevelt died, the war ended in Europe, the atom bomb was dropped, Japan surrendered, and the United Nations was organized.

In 1946 and 1947, the deluge of servicemen returning to New Orleans created a whole new set of problems. There were housing shortages, job shortages, and overcrowded colleges. But then followed the wedding boom, the baby boom, and the building boom.

A whole new era in political integrity was ushered in when veteran deLesseps S. Morrison was elected mayor in 1946. During his administration, the New Orleans Recreation Department (NORD) was created, the housing shortage dealt with, streets repaired, overpasses and underpasses built, and plans put into action to complete the new Civic Center Complex and the Union Passenger Terminal.

On the style scene, the New Look, introduced by Christian Dior, took skirt hems to new lengths and offered women unlimited amounts of fabric in their dresses. Shoes were no longer rationed, and their styles became outrageous to flatter what could be seen of the leg under these longer frocks. New Orleans was slow to respond to the new styles, but by the end of the decade, even *our* ladies were discarding most of their skimpy wartime suits and following the parade of long skirts.

It was a decade when New Orleans changed from a peacetime to a wartime economy and back again, and all inconveniences were endured with good grace and cooperation, patriotism and courage.

And on the front porches after dinner, even in 1949, ladies still sat "before the door," swatting their palmetto fans and chatting with their neighbors. At the end of the first half of the century, New Orleans, despite its beautiful new overpasses, was still just an overgrown country town. And that was the way we liked it.

MARY LOU WIDMER

Acknowledgments

I GRATEFULLY ACKNOWLEDGE the help I received in collecting information for this book from Colonel Francis E. Thomas at the Jackson Barracks Military Museum, Ron ("Mr. Football") Gaspar, sportswriter Pete Finney, baseball historian Arthur Schott, former AAU Boxing Champion Chester Banta, musicians Joe Arrigo and Rupert Surcouf, former television director Paul Yacich, television commentator Mel Leavitt, former baseball player Wilfred Theard, photographer James Lemoine of Louisiana Power and Light, the Historic New Orleans Collection archivists, all the veterans whose stories I told in chapter 7, and all the helpful librarians in the Louisiana Division of the Public Library. I am in your debt.

Also many thanks to friends and acquaintances who loaned me treasured pictures, which others may now enjoy.

Overhead view of Canal Street at the corner of Bourbon, looking toward the river.
(Courtesy The Historic New Orleans Collection, Museum/Research Center, Acc. No. 1988.31.147)

New Orleans
Orleans
⋙ in the ⋘
FORTIES

The Granada Theater, corner of Baronne and Philip streets, showed Wallace Beery coming in 20-Mule Team (1940). (Courtesy Rene Burnet)

CHAPTER ONE

A Beautiful New Decade

NEW ORLEANS ROLLED into the forties as smoothly as a night train crossing a state border. Nothing changed but the calendar. Robert Maestri had been mayor for four years and would continue in office for another six. Franklin D. Roosevelt had been president for eight years, and there was talk that he might run again for an unprecedented third term. Even the Catholic church, a strong force in the city, had been under the leadership of Archbishop Joseph Francis Rummel since 1935, and would continue to be for many years to come. Nothing moved swiftly in the Crescent City.

When the bells rang at midnight on January 1, 1940, the Great Depression had not yet ended, but unemployment had been reduced by Roosevelt's PWA and WPA. Prohibition had been repealed, and gangland murder had become little more than a memory. Things were better for most Americans but they were far from perfect.

We knew, of course, that the German Nazi dictator Adolf Hitler had sent his goose-stepping troops into Poland the previous September, engaging in the first real bloodshed of the European conflict, but New Orleanians were not too concerned about the foreign war. We tried not to think about it. Like Americans everywhere, we called ourselves Isolationists, or America Firsters.

On January first of the New Year, Tulane fans were a lot more concerned about whether "Jarrin'" John Kimbrough of Texas A & M would jar the Tulane Green Wave out of a victory in the Sugar Bowl game. Their money was on the Greenies' 160-pound scatback, Bobby ("Jitterbug") Kellogg, who they hoped could save the day. The game had been touted as a "David and Goliath" match, with A & M in the role of Goliath.

Hotel owners and restaurateurs scowled over their cash registers, wishing the Mid-Winter Sports Association had invited two out-of-town teams, which would have doubled their tourist dollars.

In homes all over the city, children slept late and then enjoyed the holiday, reading their favorite comic strips: *L'il Abner, Boots 'n Her Buddies, Toots 'n Casper,* and *Scorchy Smith.* Adults read the section in the *Times-Picayune* where the columnist Lucie Neville predicted that the best bets for stardom in the coming year were Mary Martin, Betty Field, William Holden, Robert Cummings, Linda Darnell, Lana Turner, and luscious Brenda Marshall, slated to star opposite Errol Flynn in *The Sea Hawk*.

At noon, families gathered around the dinner table to enjoy the traditional New Orleans meal, which included cabbage (for money in the New Year) and black-eyed peas (for luck). Some dined out at the new St. Regis Restaurant on Airline Highway or at Lenfant's on Canal Boulevard, and then danced to the music of the jukebox playing "I'll Never Smile Again" or "Apple Blossom Time." After the midday meal, those who were not sports fans were queuing up at the neighborhood theaters to see *Charlie Chan in Panama* with Sidney Toler, *I Want a Divorce* with Dick Powell and Joan Blondell, or *Strike Up the Band* with Mickey Rooney and Judy Garland.

There was a lot to do in New Orleans for those who had the money. At the Municipal Auditorium, Alfred Lunt and Lynn Fontaine were playing in *The Taming of the Shrew*. And at the Fair Grounds Race Track, post time was 2:15 P.M. and general admission was forty cents.

Few were thinking about American involvement in the war. They felt secure in the knowledge that the United States had signed a series of Neutrality Acts, that President Roosevelt had promised that our boys would not be sent into battle, and that men like Senator William E. Borah were calling the trouble in Europe a "phony war." To a young teenager like me, 1940 gave every promise of excitement, with new hairdos and fashions, music and dancing, and hopefully, boys and dating. As a junior in high school, I was not yet dating, but I was working on it. War, I must confess, was the farthest thing from my mind.

COLDEST MONTH ON RECORD

On January 3, tarpaulins covered plants and flowers all over the city in preparation for the season's first subfreezing weather. A temperature of thirty degrees was predicted. In the next thirty days, the city would endure its coldest weather in the history of the weather bureau.

AN ORDINARY DAY

On an ordinary schoolday, my friend Audrey and I rode the St. Claude streetcar to Holy Angels Academy in the Ninth Ward, dressed in our convent uniforms of white sport shirts, navy blue pleated skirts, saddle oxfords, and bobby sox. In a crowded streetcar, we got to sneak a peek at a few good-looking boys from Holy Cross High School who rode the same car to their campus a mile past our own, and to smile at them if we were bold enough. This brought on fits of giggling and book-dropping, but it was an exhilarating way to begin a day.

Oh, what rollicking, frolicking trolleys those St. Claude streetcars were! Flirting carried us to and from our destinations, pumping us full of adrenalin for the day, and indeed preparing us for the glorious boy-girl connections we so coveted. It was all innocent enough, of course. Sophomores dared not even talk to boys. Juniors timidly answered their questions. But something miraculous happened to girls in the summer before their senior year of high school. Suddenly, they found it easier to carry on mile-long conversations with Holy Cross boys, sometimes

The St. Claude streetcar in the early 1940s, where Holy Cross and Holy Angels students "made connections."

Boarding a streetcar and getting a transfer. (Courtesy Louisiana Power & Light)

even football players, talks which often resulted in invitations to Holy Cross dances or boatrides on the steamer *President*.

Besides the daily classes and brown-bag lunches on the tree-shaded campus, our school offered choral singing, which Audrey and I adored. My favorite after-school activity was writing for the Marianite newspaper. On rainy days at lunchtime, we all gathered in the upstairs auditorium, moved the chairs to one side, and paired off to dance the jitterbug while Dora Arroya played all the fast songs like "Hold Tight" and "Boogie Woogie Bugle Boy" on the piano.

After school each day, Audrey and I rode the streetcar to Canal Street, where we were supposed to transfer to the Cemeteries streetcar for the second half of our journey home. Instead, we spent an hour each day perusing the wares of the gigantic new Woolworth Five-and-Dime on Canal and Rampart. It was *our* store, built the first year we were in high school. There, we could look at Tangee lipsticks, compacts of Coty's powder, and tiny bottles of Blue Waltz perfume at ten cents a bottle—the treasures of the Orient to us. The shining tiled floors of the aisles beckoned us. We loved Woolworth's.

Every afternoon found us at the soda fountain there, wolfing down slices of chocolate cake with vanilla ice cream (ten cents) and regaling the waitresses with tall tales. We told them we were twins, not identical but fraternal (we did not resemble each other at all). We said we had been born in France and spoke French fluently, and then, having ascertained that they knew no French, rattled off the Our Father and Hail Mary in French, in small conversational segments, as if we were talking to each other or asking them questions. We knew the prayers by heart from our French class. The waitresses seemed mesmerized by us. We thought they were impressed. I now believe they thought us demented and were trying to be kind.

One day, we stayed at Woolworth's too long and the time on our streetcar transfers expired. We tried to bluff our way in, but the conductor put us off the car. So there we were on Canal Street without a penny in our purses, and no way to get home.

"Let's go to Paw's office," I suggested. "It's just a block away. He'll lend us carfare."

We trudged to the Audubon Building and the office of my grandfather. He was a German watchmaker of wide renown, I was later to discover. But to me he was Paw, the little old man who lived upstairs in my father's duplex, who wore bow ties and smoked cigars and put wine in his soup.

We explained our predicament. He smiled behind his gray soupstrainer moustache and drew a little coin purse from his trouser pocket. With his long fingernails, he picked out a quarter.

"Two bits enough?" he asked, obviously pleased as punch that we had come to him. Paw always counted money in "bits."

"That'll be swell," I answered. "We'll pay you back."

Carfare was seven cents each, I calculated. That would leave us eleven cents for jelly beans to eat on the way home. After leaving his office, we made a beeline to Kress, next door to the Audubon Building, and bought our jelly beans.

Of course, we never paid him back. And what was worse, we were now convinced that it made the old man so happy to lend us the money that we never bothered to check the time on our transfers after that. We lingered at Wool-worth's, trying on the jewelry and bandanas and crocheted gloves to our hearts' content, and if we were late on our transfers, we just paid Paw a visit.

LIFE WAS GOOD TO TEENAGERS

Life was good to us in the early months of 1940. We had only an occasional date to a downtown movie by way of the streetcar, but we slept over at each other's houses, and amused ourselves trying out the new pageboy hairdos and looking through magazines, admiring the strapless evening dresses. We longed for the day when we'd fill out enough to have something to hold them up. We went on occasional chaperoned truckrides to Packenham Oaks in Chalmette, and to all-day school dances on the steamer *President*.

Val Barbara's Band played for the high school boatrides on the *President*, and we adored his renditions of Glenn Miller's latest hits. I remember the huge, magnificent ladies' dressing rooms on the boat, done in art deco with a preponderance of blue mirrors, which were all the rage. Our mothers sometimes came, carrying a big picnic lunch. They watched from the upstairs balcony as we jitterbugged the day away. Those were good days, and no thoughts of war intruded to diminish their glory.

Al Hogan's orchestra played for high school dances. Back row: Tony Gondolfi (piano), Ed Chaubon (bass), Frank Alessi (trumpet), Willy Rosenmeier (drums), Clem Toca (trumpet), Leo Bickham (trombone). Front row: Bos Margiotta, Joe Arrigo, Al Hogan, Joe Ello. (Courtesy Joe Arrigo)

CURRENT EVENTS

Then one day in September, we were assigned a debate in history class. The motion on the positive was that Franklin D. Roosevelt should run for a third term; on the negative: he should not. Audrey was on the team for the positive. I was on the negative. We asked my father to help us.

By 1940, Daddy had changed his voter registration. Now he was a Republican. (In 1932, he had voted for Roosevelt.) He could give me a dozen reasons why Roosevelt should *not* run. But Audrey wanted his help, too. So Daddy, who was a walking encyclopedia of current events, reluctantly came up with a few points in favor of a third term.

We spent a whole Sunday afternoon in the living room with my father, talking Roosevelt and Isolationism, and discussing the possibility of getting into the war sooner or later. It frightened me when my father explained that although Roosevelt had promised again and again that our boys would not be sent into any foreign wars, he had asked Congress in his State of the Union message in January for funds to finance the biggest peacetime military buildup in the history of our country.

Inspired by a captive audience, my father told us that as far back as 1938, Hitler had demanded the annexation of Czechoslovakia's Sudetenland, a land rich in mines, industry, and fortifications. British Prime Minister Chamberlain had made three visits to Germany, always trying to appease the dictator. Britain and France had no heart for battle. It had been only twenty years since they had lost millions of men in what was still called the Great War. Finally, Chamberlain and French Premier Deladier gave in to Hitler's demands at Munich and, in September 1938, Czechoslovakia lost the Sudetenland to Germany. Chamberlain returned to England saying that the pact meant "peace for our time."

My father felt strongly that if France and England had acted five or six years earlier, Hitler would not have been a threat in 1940, and America's help might not be needed in the future.

Later in 1938, he said, France and England had pledged their support to Poland. By then, France had built the Maginot Line to defend against Hitler's assault, and assembled the greatest army in Europe, or so they thought. Then in September 1939, a German army of a million men, with tank divisions and the most powerful air force in Europe, invaded Poland at dawn. Before noon, Poland had become the first European country to experience the blitzkrieg (lightning war).

In fifteen days, the Nazis had conquered western Poland. Russia took this opportunity to cross Poland's Eastern Frontier, and Poland collapsed under the force of the two invading armies. Germany and Russia then signed an agreement of friendship, and divided Poland between them.

"Where were England and France all this time?" I asked.

"They declared war against Germany two days after the invasion of Poland," my father said, "but since they were unable to help at the Eastern Front, they hoped that this would draw German troops to the Western front. But the Nazis conquered Poland anyway.

"Last April, the Nazis took Denmark in just a few hours. They took Norway in just a few days. And then they marched through France, victorious. You saw it on the newsreel, the French people crying, the troops marching down the Champs Elysées."

"But what happened to the Maginot Line?" I asked, caught up in the incredible tale of conquest.

"It didn't stop Hitler. The French and the English armies joined to fight him, but in two weeks, they were retreating toward the beaches of Dunkirk."

I remembered then a Sunday afternoon when Audrey and I had sat in the flickering light of the Carrollton Theater, watching a newsreel that showed the courageous evacuation of Dunkirk in British rescue ships, including fishing boats and motor boats.

"It was just last June that the Nazis occupied Paris," my father said. "An armistice was signed between France and Germany. The rest of the French army was demobilized.

"Hitler hates the Jews," my father said, moving on to another aspect of the Nazi menace. "He's making life unbearable for them. His storm troopers have destroyed their places of business. They have no work, no place to live, no citizenship. Many have already refugeed to France and England for protection."

We listened, caring suddenly, chiding ourselves for our past frivolousness.

The school debate was held, and the juniors of Holy Angels Academy voted that Roosevelt should have no third term. Somehow he was still elected in November, defeating Wendell Willkie, a last-minute choice of the Republicans. For the first time in our history, a president would serve more than eight years.

KNITTIN' FOR BRITAIN

Close on the heels of our debate came another event that raised our consciousness level one more notch. A British lady spoke to the student body about the Battle of Britain. She told us of bombs that had been falling on London since July. She described suburbs covered by rubble, where lovely homes and gardens had been demolished. She spoke of air-raid sirens and people running for hastily dug shelters or subways, of children crying and the sky exploding with light as anti-aircraft weapons fought the German *Luftwaffe* (air force) to prevent destruction of the city.

Many English people were homeless and without food or clothing, she said, and she had come to visit schools all over America to ask for canned goods and used clothing. More than that, she had come to teach us to knit, of all things. Audrey and I looked at each other and shrugged. Although we and our friends would normally have giggled at the idea, no one did. We were deeply moved.

She wanted us to learn to knit warm socks, gloves, and scarves for the homeless who were about to endure a bitter winter without shelter. Our hearts went out to our British cousins, and we sat in quiet little groups as she came around with knitting needles and yarn, giving lessons in knitting and purling to eager young fingers. Before long we were spending our lunch hours "knittin' for Britain," proudly comparing our socks and gloves, which the nuns were to mail on for us. We were becoming involved in the war effort.

OTHER TEENAGE PURSUITS

I began reading the newspapers a bit more carefully and discovered that, while in 1939 the United States had stopped all shipments of American arms to warring nations, later on it allowed the Allies to buy goods on a "cash and carry" basis. England, however, had no more funds and China, in a life-and-death struggle with Japan, was also out of money. In September 1940, the United States gave Britain fifty overage destroyers in exchange for the right to lease military bases in Bermuda, Newfoundland, and the British West Indies. Roosevelt considered it the best land deal since the Louisiana Purchase. He asked the United States to become the "great arsenal of democracy," and to supply war materials to the Allies through sale, loan, or lease.

This was heavy reading for a junior in high school. To me, it was like algebra—hard to understand and boring, but something I would not be allowed to get by without knowing. But 1941 was coming, and in the spring, we'd be going to our Junior-Senior Prom. My heart leapt at the very thought of it, and the dismal prospect of an ever-approaching war was forgotten.

Who would I ask to be my date? I had no special boyfriend as yet. What kind of dress would I have Mrs. Scott, my neighborhood seamstress, make for me? I began sketching long-waisted, full-skirted dresses in the back of my history notebook.

As 1940 ended, Mother read aloud to me from Dorothy Kilgallen's column about the popular novel *Kitty Foyle*. "*Kitty Foyle*, by Christopher Morley," she read, "is the most daring novel ever written by a man about a woman. No woman would ever admit what it reveals.'"

She looked up and we locked eyes. She had my attention. And since the novel was serialized in the daily paper, I wasted no time sneaking it to my room and reading it. Although the love scenes were not the explicit sex scenes of today, and I was never quite sure what Kitty and her lover were doing, I got the picture when she turned up pregnant and unmarried. It was the first illicit love affair I had ever read, and I cried my eyes out and enjoyed it thoroughly.

Another column in the newspaper which my mother read daily was "Contract Bridge: How to Play and How to Win," by Josephine Culbertson. Until Culbertson arrived on the scene, we had all played auction bridge in my family. We were all avid cardplayers, and mother was now teaching us contract.

DECEMBER BROUGHT
CHRISTMAS AND TAXES

In December 1940, the newspapers said that income taxes would go up to support the defense budget. It was to be called the Victory Tax, but in spite of that, it agitated both Republicans and Isolationists. Another distressing bit of news was that the 1 percent sales tax, which was to expire at the end of the year, would be replaced by a 2 percent sales tax, to be collected in brackets. There would be no tax up to 13 cents; one cent tax for purchases of 13 cents to 62 cents; two cents tax for purchases of 63 to 99 cents. It was the subject of conversation everywhere. How could middle-class people afford such high taxes?

Christmas music and decorations in the stores took everyone's mind off war and taxes. Audrey and I fairly jigged down the aisles of Woolworth's to the tune of "Deck the Halls" as we searched the counters for gifts. We had been saving our nickels and quarters, and we each had enough money for small gifts for the members of our immediate families.

I bought my mother a brown leather purse, all gift-wrapped in a see-through box for 50 cents. My daddy and my Memere got handkerchiefs (25 cents each). For my older brother, I bought a belt for 50 cents; for my younger sister, paper dolls at 25 cents; and for my younger brother, a football, 39 cents. I completed my Christmas shopping all in one day, and it had cost me less than $2.25, tax included.

For 1940, *Rebecca* was picked as the best movie. Other movies mentioned were *Edison the Man*, *The Philadelphia Story*, *Grapes of Wrath*, *Our Town*, and *Abe Lincoln in Illinois*. And as the year came to a close, the city once again welcomed its Sugar Bowl visitors. This time fans came from out of town to cheer for the Boston College and Tennessee teams. The Mid-Winter Sports Association had made the hotel owners and restaurateurs very happy.

Tony Almerico's Band: Freddie Neuman, Joe Layacano, Frank Federico, Johnny Castaing, Tony Almerico, Charlie Miller, and Tony Costa. (Courtesy Joanne Almerico Dutfu)

CHAPTER TWO

Before the Bombs Fell

By 1941, MY FAMILY had been living in a duplex on the Orleans Canal for fourteen years, with my father's parents and sister in the upstairs apartment and my mother's parents downstairs. Much had happened in that span of time. My father's mother passed away, and so did my mother's father. My aunt married the handsome Swedish boarder who'd been with us from the start. And my mother had now had a total of five children, one of whom died at birth.

So we were four children in the house. Bob was the oldest (almost sixteen) and I was second, fourteen years old. Stock's Amusement Park had been torn down, and the neighborhood had built up considerably. Orleans Street on our side of the canal was still a narrow, rutted dirt road, but the other side had been improved and widened to accommodate growing traffic. The canal was not yet filled in.

We no longer went on family picnics to Barataria and Slidell as we had when I was small. My father was older and he had wearied of slapping mosquitoes and chasing the ants off the potato salad. And as in most families in the forties, what Daddy wanted was what everybody did. To Bob and me, it wouldn't have mattered anyway. We had better things to do with our Sundays, like going out with a date or with friends to a movie or the beach.

My widowed grandmother now shared a bedroom with my sister Elaine and me, and my two brothers occupied the third bedroom. Bob and I got along with our parents as well as most teenagers who are chomping at the bit to drive a car, to go out on dates, to have money to spend, to have no curfew, and to experience a first kiss, a first highball, a first cigarette, a first strapless evening gown, all without parental interference. Like other teenagers, we wished that our parents could have rented a nice cottage on the moon.

THE THREAT OF WAR

In March of 1941, President Roosevelt's Lend-Lease bill became law. In the next four years, the United States would send $50 billion worth of war materials to the Allies. People said FD (as he was then called in the newspapers) was

27

President Franklin D. Roosevelt explains "Lend-Lease" to Americans over radio, 1941.

The New Orleans Division of Consolidated Vultee Aircraft Corporation turned out planes like these in World War II.

drawing us into the war. He responded that he'd keep war away from our shores for all times. This he did, but not without drawing us into the war.

In his fireside chats, Roosevelt explained the necessity of sending the needed supplies to England, the last bastion against the Nazis before the Atlantic Ocean and our own shores. He urged that there be no strikes and no profiteering, so that England might get the tanks, guns, and supplies she needed so badly.

After the Lend-Lease Law, Hitler said he'd attack all ships bringing supplies to Britain. Italians were deported from the United States, and Californians cast an anxious eye upon the Japanese-Americans in their midst. It was another World War, no doubt about that, and people were beginning to label it World War II.

OUR JUNIOR-SENIOR PROM

But here in New Orleans, at Holy Angels Academy, an event that Audrey and I considered of equal importance was drawing near, and it demanded all our attention. Our Junior-Senior Prom was coming in May! Mother and I shopped for fabric at D. H. Holmes. We selected a pale blue organdy eyelet material, yards and yards of it, and a pattern for a sleeveless, long-waisted evening dress with a sweetheart neckline and a skirt wide enough to accommodate two starched petticoats.

In school, votes were taken for a band and a place to hold the prom. The vote went to Tony Almerico's Band, a group of fantastic musicians. The location we voted for was the Southern Yacht Club, on the West End Park peninsula, at the point where the New Basin Canal empties into Lake Pontchartrain. It is the second oldest yacht club in the country, with a dance floor that to me looked as big as a football field.

For my date, I asked a friend who was a good dancer, since I had no special boyfriend. The good dancers were called "solid senders," and they were very important in the scheme of things. He had to make *me* look like a good dancer, so that the boys who came "stag" would cut in on me, knowing they wouldn't get "stuck."

Each junior and senior was given four invitations: one for her escort and three for stags, who were more or less obliged to cut in on her at the prom and make her look popular.

It was all a game we played. The girls flirted, talking gaily to their partners on the dance floor, letting their long hair swing out in their wake, trying to encourage their own stags and anybody else's to line up to dance with them. The object was, of course, to look like the belle of the ball and to make the other girls *pea green with envy*, as Scarlett O'Hara would have said. The stags, for their part, took their good sweet time about it, walking around and sizing up the girls. If a boy found one he liked, he looked around him to see if there was at least one other stag waiting to dance with her so that he wouldn't have to spend the rest of the night with her. No matter how good she looked, she might turn out to be a bore.

I remember proms and student dances where I'd be stuck with the same boy so long, I'd pray to St. Jude, promising fifty cents to his poor box if he'd please let a boy cut in on me. If no boys came, I'd up the ante to one dollar, sometimes to two dollars. And once I saw a boy passing a dollar to a friend behind his partner's back—the price of releasing him from bondage.

But then there were nights like our Junior-Senior Prom in May of 1941 when everything was perfect. It was the best, and nothing before or since has ever topped it. That night, I knew my dress was a knockout, and my long pink silk gloves were just perfect, and the corsage my date had sent me didn't make me look as if I'd just won the Kentucky Derby, and my waistline looked almost invisible in the body-hugging blue eyelet dress, and my date danced me out onto the floor, twirling me under his uplifted arm, making me look so great that a line formed at once and replenished itself all night. I felt like Cinderella at the ball.

The Southern Yacht Club, second oldest in the United States and scene of many high schools proms in the forties. (Courtesy The Historic New Orleans Collection, Museum/Research Center, Acc. No. 1979.325.6397)

Special DeLuxe 1941 Plymouth. What a car!

THE SUMMER OF '41—
WHERE TO GO ON DATES

The summer before our senior year worked the predictable miracle on Audrey and me. We grew up. We filled out, at least to an acceptable degree. We became more comfortable in the presence of boys. We dated more, now even in cars. Audrey and I and our dates often doubled, but my mother felt more secure if I doubled with my brother, and we were amenable to that whenever we were able to get each other dates. I decided that it was very nice to have a brother the same age as the boys I dated.

One popular place for young people to go on dates was O'Shaugnessy's Bowling Alley on Airline Highway. It was an enormous place with miles of bowling lanes and pool tables in the back. We all soon learned how to score and developed a rudimentary technique. Many a Friday night was spent there, and sometimes, after a movie, we'd stop in for a quick game.

Another place that drew us like a magnet was Pontchartrain Beach Amusement Park, which had been moved to the end of Elysian Fields Avenue at Lake Pontchartrain in 1939. It had formerly been located on Bayou St. John at the lake, an area that was now part of the Lake Vista residential subdivision.

The rides were inexpensive, and the Penny Arcade was a delight to teenagers. There was always a free show if you arrived before nine o'clock. Aerial artists, magicians, and dancers entertained us at the Beach, and once a year, the bathing beauty contest brought New Orleanians by the thousands to the lakefront.

The Zephyr was the park's symbol. Its speed was terrifying and the plunge down the first dip was heart-stopping (all the better to make you throw your arms around your date's neck). We loved the "Cockeyed Circus," a crazy house you walked through while puffs of wind blew your skirt up over your head and barrels threatened to fall on you, all to the accompaniment of a fat lady laughing incessantly on a record.

Already at Pontchartrain Beach, men in uniform were beginning to dot the crowd. Some of them were stationed at the Naval Reserve Aviation Base adjacent to the amusement center on the lakefront. In time this area would include an Aircraft Carrier Training Center and a Rest and Recreation Area, a tent city where servicemen on leave were sent to relax. Other servicemen came from Camp Leroy Johnson on the eastern side of the amusement park. They were all just boys away from home, and they enjoyed the amusements of Pontchartrain Beach, which was in walking distance of their military installations. The war was beginning to cut a design into the lakefront.

Another good place to go on a date was West End Park, with its fountain of many colors. It was situated in an oval of land surrounded by outdoor seafood restaurants where we ate crabs and drank cold draft beer as the lakefront breezes riffled our hair.

OPERATION BARBAROSSA

June 22, 1941, more than 150 German and other Axis divisions swept across the Russian border, turning on their former ally in Operation Barbarossa. Three million Germans faced two million Russian troops, and the battle line stretched 2,000 miles, from the Arctic to the Black Sea. Hitler announced that he was saving the entire world from bolshevism, but Germany needed Russia's vast supplies of food, petroleum, and other raw materials. Hitler fully expected to effect another blitzkrieg. He made no plans for a long struggle. He did not even issue winter uniforms to his troops.

We saw it in the RKO Radio News at the Carrollton, the five weeks of fighting in which the Germans drove the Russians back, taking thousands of prisoners. The collapse of Russia was expected at any moment. But as the Germans advanced, the Russians destroyed everything in their path: factories, dams, railroads, and food supplies. Great Britain and the United States shipped lend-lease supplies to Russia through the Arctic Ocean and the Persian Gulf, and the United States began losing ships in the Arctic to German planes and submarines.

"We ought not to help either one," my father said. "Let them keep fighting till they wipe each other out and do the world a favor." Many people shared his sentiments.

ANDREW JACKSON HIGGINS,
NEW ORLEANS' OWN GREAT BOATBUILDER

Meanwhile, down in New Orleans, a small boatbuilder named Andrew Jackson Higgins, who apparently felt challenged by insoluble problems, had long been wrestling with a transportation dilemma for the man who had to make a living in the swamps. Actually, Higgins was a lumberman, but in his heart he was a boatbuilder, and had been ever since he'd built his first boat as a boy on the Missouri River in Nebraska. In 1929, his *And How III* had made the run from New Orleans to St. Louis in eighty-seven hours, and in 1930, his *Dixie Greyhound* cut the time to seventy-two hours and four minutes.

Demonstration by Higgins landing craft.

31

His current problem was how to build a ship whose propeller would not get wrapped up in water hyacinth, whose speed would not be diminished by sandbars, and whose bottom would not be ripped apart by sunken stumps. Higgins and his crew went to work on it. Their plans began to take shape, and at last, they knew they had the answer.

The *Eureka*, they called it, and it jumped over floating logs and sandbars without even slowing down. It climbed smoothly onto dry land, and even a ride up a concrete seawall couldn't damage its tough bottom. Wherever you beached it, it could spin around under its own power.

Higgins Industries City Park plant during World War II.

The World War II production line of cargo ships at the Higgins Industrial Canal plant.

Higgins ramp-landing boat in practice landing.

The *Eureka* made Higgins famous. It could fly through the swamps, going where no power craft had ever been before. The demand for these boats grew, and Higgins could not open new shops fast enough to keep up with it. Orders came from oilmen, since many Louisiana oil fields are under water or in marshland.

In the summer of '41, before the United States entered the war, the British were using Higgins boats in the English Channel. They were enjoying the speed and maneuverability of the combat craft designed by the New Orleans boatbuilder, whose plants had now become the largest in the world. And these feats in the English Channel were but dress rehearsals for the larger landings that would later turn the tide of the war in favor of the Allies. A few years later, Higgins' spoonbill prow pushed its way up the beaches of Africa and the Mediterranean. It dropped men and tanks on the enemies' shores, then backed up and spun around to be off before the next surf came rolling in.

Although the Higgins plant on City Park Avenue was only four blocks away from our home on the Orleans Canal, and we passed it almost every day, we knew nothing of its heroic achievements. That was necessarily clothed in secrecy, like many another military project in the city.

As time went on, Higgins' plants turned out not only tugboats and barges, amphibious equipment, and cargo ships but patented devices used by other boatbuilders. Among their products were cargo-carrying "flying box cars," produced in the Higgins Aircraft Plant in Higgins, Louisiana, the largest building of its kind in the world under one roof. Connected to the plant was the largest privately owned airport on earth. Andrew Jackson Higgins made history in the boatbuilding industry in World War II.

Defense work in the shipbuilding industry got many New Orleanians off the WPA rolls, men who had been working for mere sustenance wages. It was logical that many of the navy's vessels would be built here. We had the climate, the natural resources—oil, gas, sulphur, and timber—a good labor supply, and water transportation through the Mississippi Valley to all parts of the world.

Planes for our armed forces abroad being loaded onto our Victory Fleet.

BUCK PRIVATES,
A MOVIE ABOUT THE PEACETIME ARMY

One upbeat, lighthearted movie showing mock battles in the peacetime army was *Buck Privates*, with Bud Abbott and Lou Costello. It was a hilarious comedy calculated to increase voluntary enlistments and to make potential draftees less anxious. The Andrews Sisters, with their incomparable harmony, played WAACs (members of the Women's Army Auxiliary Corps, later shortened to WACs) who sang a few jivey new songs like "You're in the Army, Mr. Jones," "Boogie Woogie Bugle-Boy of Company B," and the deliciously beautiful "I'll Be with You in Apple Blossom Time."

SENIORS GOT SPECIAL PRIVILEGES

September came to New Orleans and with the start of the school year, all thoughts of war vanished from our minds. The Holy Cross-Holy Angels streetcars rolled again, much to the chagrin, I'm sure, of the streetcar conductors. The flirting began again. This was our big year. We were seniors, the Class of '42. We had paid our dues and the reward for our first three years of shyness and intimidation was a sudden, surprising self-confidence and boldness. We not only talked to the Holy Cross boys now, but we were selective about it. In our newfound narcissism, we had become particular about whom we conversed with. Soon we were sporting class rings, gold with royal blue stones etched with the school's letters, AHA. We were hot stuff, and didn't we know it!

Seniors, as we'd always known, were assigned all the choice jobs and awarded all the honors—editor of the Marianite newspaper, publisher of the yearbook, leading stars in Mother Xavier's annual pageant, Student Council officers, and prefect of the Sodality. And this was rightly so, we thought, now that we were seniors. Audrey and I accepted the honors due us. Audrey was selected by Mother Xavier to address the archbishop on his visit to the school. I was secretary of the Sodality, and I played the part of Mary Magdalene in the Passion play Mother Xavier wrote that year.

Every year, Mother Mary Francis Xavier, the provincial superior of the Southern Province of the Sisters of the Holy Cross, who lived in her private bedroom on the third floor of our high school building, wrote, directed, and produced a pageant, which we rehearsed all year to perform in the spring. This year it was to be a Passion play, something she had planned for a long time. For it she wrote the entire musical score, which she herself played on the organ. I truly believe she would have taken a crack at playing all the parts if she had been allowed to dispense with her habit.

UNDECLARED WAR

As early as September 1941, the *Item* newspaper told of Air Warning Centers being set up where civilians could be on the lookout for enemy planes. The war was drawing near. Hitler continued to bomb British cities, he overran the Balkan countries, and his troops in Russia were beginning to feel the bite of a Russian winter. American warships were convoying supplies partway to England, and the United States found itself in a state of undeclared war with Germany.

Avondale Marine Ways, a vital defense-vessel manufacturer during the war.

A Liberty ship built by our Delta Shipyards.

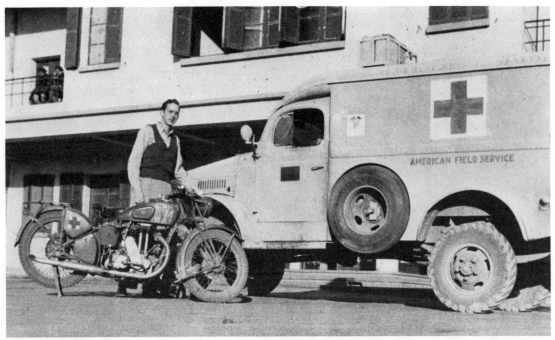

American Field Service ambulance presented by New Orleans Public Service.
(Courtesy Louisiana Power & Light)

In September of 1940, Japan had landed in Indochina and let the world know that it wanted control of the Pacific. General Douglas MacArthur, commander-in-chief of the army in the Philippines, was mobilizing for defense in case of war. American factories were rallying for national defense. And in October, Lieutenant-General Hideki Tojo of Japan threatened the United States to stop sending aid to China, *or else.* In November 1941, Secretary of State Hull met with Tojo's special representatives, Saburo Kuruso and Kichi-saburo Nomura, to discuss American aid to China and the presence of Japanese troops in Indochina. But the Japanese cabinet had already accepted Tojo's decision to go to war against the United States.

The declaration of war, December 8, 1941.

CHAPTER THREE

The Day of Infamy

EVERYONE REMEMBERS EXACTLY where he was when he heard the news that Japan had bombed Pearl Harbor—everyone except me. People can tell you who they were with and what color clothes they were wearing. But I forgive myself for not having those details etched in my memory. I was only fifteen, and the real meaning of what had happened took time to sink in.

Because of the time difference between Hawaii and Pearl Harbor, the news did not come over the radio until early afternoon. My father didn't have the radio on when I left home after Sunday midday dinner to go to a movie in town with friends. As we came out of the theater and walked the two blocks to Walgreen's drugstore to have a malt, we heard the newsboys shouting, "Extra! Extra!" and then something that sounded like, "Japan bombs Pearl Harbor." What in the world did it mean, we wondered. And why were so many people rushing to buy newspapers?

It seems hard to believe but we ignored them all and had our malt. We talked about the movie we'd just seen and about upcoming Christmas parties and Christmas shopping. It wasn't until I got home and saw my almost-seventeen-year-old brother sitting on the porch, gazing thoughtfully into space, that the subject came up again.

"Did you hear the news?" he asked.

I nodded. "Yes, but I don't understand it. What's a Pearl Harbor?"

"It's not a what, dummy. It's a place," he said. "It's in Hawaii." I took no offense. He always called me "dummy," and we both understood it as a term of endearment.

"Well, what's everybody getting so excited about?"

"Because it means war, don't you get it? Hawaii belongs to the United States. It's the same as if they'd bombed New Orleans or New York. It's a declaration of war."

"Oh, my God!" I sank down onto the porch glider. Weakness washed over me. "Has the president talked on the radio about it?"

"No, but he will tomorrow morning. Dad says he has no choice. We'll have to go to war."

War! I couldn't believe it. Sending all our young boys overseas to fight the Japanese! All along, we'd been thinking of Germany as the enemy, not Japan. Why had *they* attacked us? Hadn't the papers shown pictures of Japanese envoys in conference with Cordell Hull and President Roosevelt just a few days ago?

I looked at Bob, who had fallen silent again. He was thinking of the war, of course. He would be seventeen in January. Could it last long enough for him to be drafted?

A STATE OF WAR EXISTS

In the next few days, our worst fears were confirmed. The following day, the president announced that on December 7, 1941, "a date which will live in infamy," the Empire of Japan had ruthlessly attacked Pearl Harbor and that, since that time, a state of war had existed between the United States and Japan.

The details were soon in all the newspapers. While Japanese emissaries had been negotiating with Hull, a thirty-three-ship Japanese fleet had been steaming eastward. And then, on December 7, at 7:55 Hawaii time, 360 Japanese airplanes attacked the naval base at Pearl Harbor, the army aircraft at Hickam Field, and other nearby military installations. Two hours later, the United States had lost the battleships *Arizona*, *California*, *Oklahoma*, and *West Virginia*, the mine layer *Oglala*, and the target ship *Utah*, as well as 174 planes. Damaged were three battleships, three cruisers, and three destroyers. The Japanese attack had dealt the United States a crippling blow. That same day, the Japanese government had declared war on the United States and Britain, and on December 8, we heard the president declare war against Japan. Then on December 11, Germany and Italy declared war against the United States, and Congress then declared war on Germany and Italy.

"Why was Germany so obliging?" my father asked at the dinner table that night. "They didn't have to declare war on us. The United States was still divided as to whether or not it should go to war against the Nazis. Hitler thinks he's a Superman, but how many enemies does he think he can fight at one time?

"Well," he added, "he's cut his own throat now."

We were all silent after that. We weren't sure what that meant, exactly. And in spite of how well informed my father was, he couldn't possibly know how it would all end. No one could, but we were in it now for good. It would be the biggest war in the history of the world, and for the next three years and eight months, all our lives would be turned upside down.

There was never any opposition to the war—no antiwar movement, no pacifist doctrines. No one objected to the huge appropriations the government was requesting or even to the draft. Yet, strangely enough, there were few military parades and few voices lifted in song, as there had been in the First World War. Without hysteria, the people buckled down to work hard and get the job done. One rarely heard bands playing or trumpets blaring, rousing the men to arms. The United States had learned in 1918 that there was nothing glamorous about war.

Wives and mothers gave up their sons and husbands patriotically if not willingly, but everyone resented the new drastic government controls. And men who had been out of work during the Depression went into the army not knowing what the future held for them when they came back, *if* they came back.

In the immediate aftermath of Pearl Harbor, there was a definite vibration in the air, not unlike what we in New Orleans felt when we heard the news on the radio that a hurricane was coming. A hurricane was a fearful thing, bringing with it a terrible rush of anxieties, but there was an undeniable exhilaration in preparing for it by boarding windows and storing water in jugs and searching for candles in the bureau drawers. Neighbors helped each other get ready. They shared the news and they shared their fears, and for a brief time, they secretly enjoyed a relief from the boredom of everyday life.

That's how it was after war was declared. We hadn't gotten into the ugly part of it yet. People were still fired up with a desire to get even with the Japanese, exhilarated with the enormity of the task that lay ahead.

In the week after Pearl Harbor, many eligible men enlisted in the armed forces, and in a remarkably short time, industries announced that they would be converting from peacetime to wartime production. Plants that had made vacuum cleaners began producing machine guns. Automobile factories began producing airplanes and tanks. The plant-and-parts depot of the Ford Motor Company in Arabi, Louisiana, was leased to the War Department for the duration of the war. Japan had indeed "awakened a sleeping giant," as Admiral Isoroku Yamamoto, the architect of the Pearl Harbor plan, had said after the bombing.

LIFE AT HOME

But life went on pretty much the same for my immediate family, except that my father bought a huge world map and hung it in the hallway so that he could mark the areas of combat and follow the victories and defeats of the United States armed forces. In my own world of high school dances and dating, it was easy to forget the momentous events happening on the other side of the world, and even our own country's involvement in them.

That December, Audrey and I did our Christmas shopping as usual. We walked through the Roosevelt Hotel lobby, decorated as always like a fairyland for the Christmas holidays. Angel hair made a cavelike roof of the lobby's cathedral ceiling, and Christmas trees and ornaments lined the long corridor that crossed the block from Baronne Street to University Place.

We stared in awe at the elaborate displays in the windows of Maison Blanche and D. H. Holmes' department stores, where animated characters waved at us or rode a carousel or decorated a Christmas tree. The displays seemed to grow more detailed and more beautiful every year.

Our Christmas Eve dance was to be held at the home of Elaine and Leila de Verges, two pretty sisters who were members of our little sorority. We called it a sorority to sound grown-up, but it was just a club of about twenty-five young girls, ages fourteen to sixteen. We held meetings and paid dues, and planned dances like this one.

In Elaine and Leila's home, which was located in a lovely old section near City Park, the basement had been converted into a playroom with paneled walls, tiled floors, draperies, game tables, and a little powder room. They even had their own jukebox. I, for one, was enormously impressed.

For our dance, we were allowed to ask a boy as a date and two others as stags. What was a dance if there were no stags to cut in on you? How would you know if you were popular?

We all gave a great deal of thought to our evening dresses, which had to be memorable, at the very least. Mine was made of raspberry net over the palest blue taffeta, the two fabrics cut and sewn together as one by Mrs. Scott. It was the closest thing to strapless, having only tiny rhinestone straps on bare shoulders and back; a snug-fitting, drop-waisted bodice; and of course, an enormous skirt.

Christmas Eve came, and when the dancing was in full swing and the stag lines were forming and the jukebox was blaring out Glenn Miller's "Little Brown Jug," I saw walking toward me a handsome boy with jet black hair, green eyes, and the most enormous shoulders. He tapped my partner on the shoulder and gave me a ravishing Pepsodent smile. My partner turned away and the stranger put his arm around my waist.

"Hi!" he said. "I'm Al Widmer."

My knees went suddenly wobbly and I had to catch my breath before I spoke. I introduced myself, and we talked. I spent the rest of the night waiting for him to come back and dance with me again, and he spent the rest of the night waiting reasonable periods of time before doing so.

The girls told me in the powder room that Al Widmer was the best player on the Jesuit High School football team (this I didn't know, being a Holy Cross fan), and that he and his friend Harry, also a football player, had crashed the party. Of course, the proper thing to do was to ask them both to leave, but everyone wanted them to stay. They weren't even wearing coats or ties, for Heaven's sake. They had just walked into the basement entrance, with no invitations, wearing football jackets over sport shirts. It was hardly the way to dress for a formal party on Christmas Eve, but I prayed to God that no one would put them out. And no one did.

Al told me later that Harry knew a girl in our sorority, so he knew about the party, but she hadn't sent him an invitation. He said that he and Harry had nothing else to do on Christmas Eve, so they took a chance that they wouldn't be stopped at the door.

Al also told me months later that when he saw me on Christmas Eve, he thought I was the prettiest girl he'd ever seen. But in spite of that, and in spite of the fact that some definite signals had passed between us, I waited weeks and weeks for him to call and finally gave up waiting because he never did. I can't say it broke my heart, but it definitely injured my pride.

I forgot all about him for a while, except when I read about his athletic exploits on the sports page, where his name appeared with surprising frequency. High school sports news was big in New Orleans in the forties. This was never more

Jesuit championship 1940 backfield: Al Widmer, Leonard Finley, O. J. Key, Armand ("Rock") Roussel, and Tony diBartolo.

evident than when Al broke his thumb at football practice and it made the headlines on the sports page. But time went on and I had other dates and I did not grieve over his absence.

NO WHISTLES ON NEW YEAR'S EVE

Before the end of December 1941, the New Orleans Defense Coordinator requested that no whistles be blown on New Year's Eve. He also requested that no factory, steamship, or locomotive whistles be blown, now that whistles were to be used as air-raid sirens.

On January 13, 1941, we read a list of "Air Raid Instructions for Civilian Defense" in the *Item* newspaper:

> Stay away from windows. Glass shatters easily.
>
> Don't go to the window and look out. It's dangerous and it helps the enemy. The Air-Raid Warden is out there watching out for you.
>
> Get off the streets if planes come over. [We shivered at that one, remembering the British lady and her stories of war-torn London.] Anti-aircraft fire means falling shrapnel. You are safe from it if you're indoors, away from windows. Go there at the first alarm, and stay until the "All Clear."
>
> Stay calm. Stay home. Put out lights. Lie down. Stay away from windows. You can help lick the Japs, just with your bare hands, if you will just do these few, simple things.
>
> Be a good fellow and follow instructions and keep well. Do not be a wise guy and get hurt.

The writing style in itself is cute and funny when compared to the journalism of today. When do you ever read instructions in the newspaper now where they ask you to be a "good fellow"? But there was something homey and informal about it that made you want to follow their suggestions.

One air-raid warden who was watching out for people was my father. I'm sure he must have been the first man in the city to answer the call for block wardens, and he was never prouder in his life than when he was patrolling the block during air-raid drills, wearing his metal World War I helmet and carrying his flashlight.

Blackout instruction booklets were delivered by Boy Scouts to every house in the city. The stores were soon running ads for splinterproof blackout pads which could be hung on wall hooks over your regular draperies or curtains or shades, preventing even a sliver of light from being seen from the outside. They could be put up quickly and they offered protection from shattered glass. They sold for $2.99 or $3.99, depending on the size.

Our principal at Holy Angels mimeographed the following notice and sent it to the parents of every child in school:

> PARENTS: READ THIS
>
> If an air raid should come while your children are in school, see to your own safety. Stay home, go to your refuge room, stay away from windows.
>
> Do not try to reach the school. You could accomplish no good. You could do a great deal of harm by such action.
>
> In an air raid, Rule Number One is to stay off the street, get under cover. On the street, there is the risk of falling shell fragments, racing cars and fire apparatus. Stay indoors.
>
> Do not try to telephone. The wire must be kept clear for the wardens, the police, and the fire department. You might prevent an urgent message from getting through.
>
> This is hard advice. It is not easy to take, but it is for the best interest and for the welfare of your children.

What amazes me now is the fact that they thought that our being bombed was a distinct possibility. I wasn't too frightened then. I had never lived through a war, and I had no idea how horrible and devastating it could be.

In February, an air-raid alarm system was shown in a drawing in the paper. A few months later, it was installed, and soon we were hearing the frightening sound of the siren during drills and taking shelter in our homes as we'd been instructed.

Students began collecting books to send to our men in the armed services. "Victory" books, they were called. "Victory" was the catchword. It was a rousing word; it was a prayer.

In May, New Orleanians registered with their local ration boards to get sugar ration books. The head of the household was allowed to register for everyone in the family, but could not have more than two pounds per person on hand at any one time.

"How can they know how much sugar you have in your pantry?" I asked my mother. "No one can enforce a rule like that."

"They won't have to, honey," my mother said. "People will do it willingly." And so they did.

In restaurants, sugar bowls were taken off the tables, and individual servings were offered the customers in small glass pitchers. "In the First World War," my father said, "the restaurants gave you sugar in little paper packets, but this time, there's a shortage of paper, too."

GRADUATION: HANDKERCHIEFS
HIDE CLEAVAGE

Audrey and I graduated from Holy Angels Academy on May 30, 1942. I recall as if it were yesterday the fragrance of the American Beauty roses we held in our arms as we walked single file in our long white evening dresses up the steps of the stage in the schoolyard. Mother Xavier inspected our dresses individually, while a flunky sister followed with a stack of freshly laundered men's white linen handkerchiefs. If Mother detected the slightest hint of cleavage, she took a handkerchief from the pile and tucked it into the offending bosom. We had been

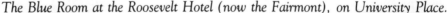

The Blue Room at the Roosevelt Hotel (now the Fairmont), on University Place.

warned not to come in strapless evening gowns, and no one dared defy that order. But the degree of decolletage was not so easy to dictate, and many a youthful bosom was at least partly in evidence . . . until Mother Xavier made her inspection.

Our Senior Prom was held at the Blue Room in the Roosevelt Hotel. A terraced section at the end of the nightclub farthest from the bandstand had been reserved for the girls and their dates. Word soon passed around that Bob Hope was at a nearby table, and we all spent the major part of the evening pestering the man for autographs and greatly resenting it when he asked us to "go home." I think it's only in very recent years that Audrey and I forgave him for not being gracious in the face of *our* bad manners. So much for youth!

A week after my graduation, in early June of 1942, I met Al Widmer again at a city-wide Sodality dance at Holy Name of Jesus auditorium (now Mercy Academy). Strange how things happen, I often think. Just suppose I'd missed the dance that night. I wonder who my children would have looked like.

But we *did* meet, six months after our first encounter, and this time, there was no mistaking how happy he was to see me. This time, he was going to make sure those vibes that were passing between us would be nurtured. He had come stag to the dance with Jerry Ford (now of Ford Models Inc. of New York), who was his buddy in football and track. Al had by this time been elected captain of the 1942–43 football, basketball, and track teams at Jesuit, a rare honor for any athlete.

Al and Jerry both rushed me at first, but then Jerry, seeing that Al was attracted to me, wandered off to dance with some other girls, and Al and I sat and talked until the dance ended. That very night, he asked me to go with him to his Jesuit Senior Prom the following week. I was delighted to learn that he hadn't been dating other girls. He'd simply been too busy with schoolwork and sports to have time to date. And money was also in short supply.

At his graduation at the Municipal Auditorium, Al received three trophies, which his mother carried home when he and I left for the prom in the University Room at the Roosevelt Hotel. He didn't take a diploma that night. He cleared up my confusion by explaining that he should have been graduating that year, 1942, just as I had, but he'd accepted Coach Gernon Brown's offer to return for a postgraduate course (something they offered in those days) so that he could play sports for Jesuit one more year.

When the plan was first proposed to him, it seemed like a great idea. With one more year of exposure, he'd be getting offers for scholarships from lots of colleges, among them, hopefully, Georgetown. It was his dream to go there, and his mother, a widow with a limited income, would not have been able to afford the tuition. But in the time since those plans had been made, everything had changed. There was a war on now and Al was already seventeen. By the time he finished his postgraduate course in 1943, he'd be eighteen and eligible for the draft. He'd probably get drafted right out of high school and never even get to go to college.

I knew him far too short a time to offer any advice, even if I'd known what was best. He had no father to advise him. And as the summer months advanced and we knew we were falling in love, he wondered if he would have gone away to college even if he'd gotten an offer from Georgetown. But in the summer of '42, we knew only that we were very much in love, that there was a terrible war on, and that Al Widmer, like many others, was heading right into it.

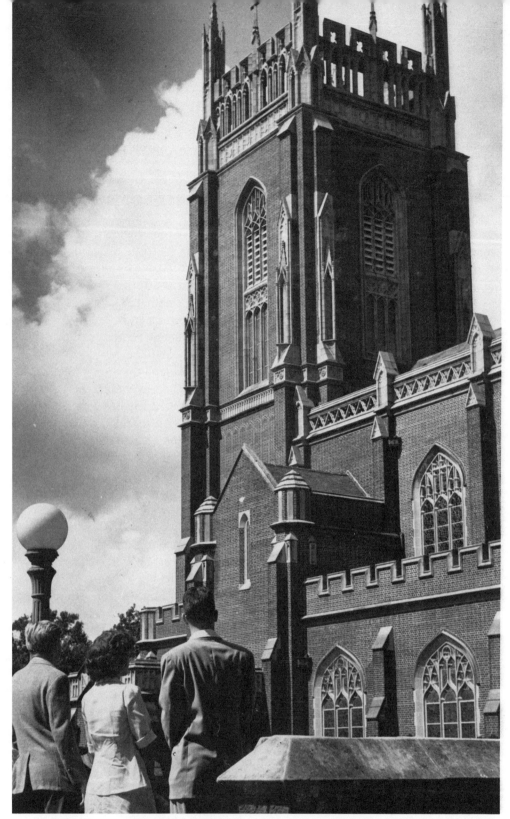

Author with two other freshmen on the first day of school at Loyola. This picture was used as the frontispiece in the 1943 yearbook.

CHAPTER FOUR

My Summer of '42

UNLIKE THE MOVIE of the same name, my "Summer of '42" did not take place in a country town with a sand beach. The setting was New Orleans, more specifically Loyola University, where I was taking History 101 and Sociology 101 in advance of my first regular semester of college. My brother's girlfriend, Vernon, and I took the same sociology class. We rode back and forth together in the streetcar, studied together, and one afternoon a week, took in a movie at the Orpheum or the Center Theater on Canal Street. We each had an allowance of $3.50 a week, and it was amazing what we could do with that pittance. Today, you couldn't even get into the movie on that.

Like the characters in *Summer of '42*, we were very much interested in romance and desperate to learn anything we could about sex. But unlike the movie characters, we had no book on anatomy and would have been too embarrassed to check one out at the library. There was virtually no source that could be tapped for this information.

Our mothers were no help at all. I can never remember the subject of sex being discussed in our house on Orleans Street. And Vernon's mother was even worse. Nice people didn't discuss such subjects. How did nice people ever have children, I wondered. Movies showed nothing more explicit than a closed-mouth kiss, and how we swooned when Clark Gable took Lana Turner in his arms in *Honky Tonk* and kissed her!

Books told us nothing. Audrey and I once read aloud to each other from the book *Deep Summer*, by Gwen Bristow, which I had pilfered from my Aunt Hazel's library, and we were so shocked that the heroine was throwing up because she was pregnant that we read the passage over and over again. That's how information-deprived we were. And I was already in college!

LOYOLA—NO LONGER
AN ALL-MALE SCHOOL

I felt privileged to be going to Loyola University. Except in its professional colleges (dentistry, pharmacy, etc.), it had always restricted its enrollment to men. But during the Depression, New Orleans Normal School, a two-year college for teachers, closed its doors. Now young women who wanted to be teachers had no place to go except Dominican College, which was overcrowded. So, for the first time, Loyola offered to take young women into the College of Arts and Sciences. But only twenty girls had been admitted the previous year, when Vernon started, and only twenty in 1942 when I started, admission being based on grades and the student's willingness to pursue a teaching career.

I had never planned to be a teacher. I wanted to be a journalist or a novelist, but I discovered that I could have a major in education and a minor in English and journalism, giving me a good foundation for both. So there we were, Vernon and I, two out of a very few girl students in a college of all boys. What a paradise! The fact that she was dating Bob and I was dating Al did not dampen our enthusiasm. We were far from ready to sign a marriage contract, and with such a sea of boys to choose from, we planned to do a little fishing.

In June of 1942, most boys were under draft age when they started college, at least in New Orleans, where there was no eighth grade. They were all sixteen or seventeen years old, and we soon learned that there was such a thing as deferment—delay of draft—under some circumstances for boys who were already in college when they reached eighteen.

One such circumstance was being in a school of dentistry or pharmacy. Another was being in the V–12 program of the navy, a program offered at Tulane University, which some of the students at Loyola were investigating. A V–12 program for the army was soon offered at Loyola. Deferment was a popular topic of conversation, but there were many boys who were eager to go to war and left college to join the military service.

FLIRTING ON CANAL STREET

One early summer day, after Vernon and I had completed our classes and taken the streetcar to town, we were walking along Canal Street at a leisurely pace, window-shopping, when hoots and catcalls attracted our attention. A group of boys were standing out in front of Kress Five-and-Dime (presently The Gap), next door to Maison Blanche, whistling at us.

"Hubba-hubba!" said one of the boys whom I did not recognize. Suddenly I spied Al Widmer. It was early on in our courtship, and we were still a little shy around each other. He was in the midst of this group, his back against the glass display window and his head was lowered in embarrassment, his ever-present smile decorating his handsome face. The other boys were nudging him and pointing in my direction. Evidently he had told them about me when he saw me coming and they were taking their chance to needle him.

I smiled nervously, took Vernon's arm, and walked as fast as I could past the laughing, taunting group. But I had never been so pleased in my life. I knew then that I was important to him, and I was elated.

I later learned that Al was working in the stockroom at Maison Blanche for the summer, at least until football practice started in August, to pick up some dating money. He and his friends—I have no idea where *they* were working—met on their lunch hour in front of Kress to watch the girls go by.

From that day on, no matter what else our plans were for the afternoon, Vernon and I walked past Kress at 12:30. The boys were always there, but we never stopped. Al and I never spoke, but we exchanged smiles and glances. My heart raced, and it made my day. Neither one of us ever missed the noon encounter.

On June 3, the Battle of Midway began. The United States had cracked the Japanese naval code, enabling Admiral Nimitz to launch aircraft from three U.S. carriers, meeting and defeating the Japanese planes launched from their own carriers. When the battle ended on June 6, Japan had lost four carriers and many planes, ending their expansion eastward to Hawaii and the United States. It was one of the most decisive victories in history.

CHEAP DATES AND DOUBLE DATES

Al started calling me at night and coming over to my house for "cheap" dates. We took long walks in City Park and stopped for snowballs at the Casino. We sometimes walked to Canal near Carrollton to an outdoor stand with tables and benches, where you could sit and enjoy a cold slice of watermelon for twenty-five cents.

On Saturday nights, we double-dated either with Audrey and her date, whoever that might be (she was very popular), or with Bob and Vernon. If we went with Bob, we traveled in his old Hudson Terraplane, which used a tankful of gas on the trip from City Park to Lakeview, and which we always wound up pushing home. He had bought the car secondhand with money he'd made selling shoes part time at Chandler's Shoe Store on Canal Street near Dauphine, and he'd gotten stuck with a lemon.

To digress for a moment, Bob was an interesting brother. He never let any grass grow under his feet. He had had a paper route since he was twelve, and now that he was seventeen, he worked every spare hour at Chandler's. Because he was such a good salesman, he was allowed to come into Chandler's to sell whenever he liked. He had no set part-time days. He concentrated on selling PMs. These were shoes that didn't move, usually because they weren't stylish. He pushed them at every chance because they earned him an extra commission. He told the ladies that they were the finest shoes ever manufactured, and they believed him.

Besides having more than his share of baloney, he was good-looking and unfailingly neat. The customers loved him. We used to say that Bob could sell snowshoes in Africa. And it proved prophetic, since he later had his own advertising agency and made a very good living at selling.

Bob got good grades in school without ever opening a book. If he had studied, he would have been dangerous. In addition to this, he was funny. He had a wonderful sense of humor and he was a fabulous artist. Artistic talent ran in our family, but it never even brushed by me. Bob had been taking art lessons at Hans Wang Art School on St. Peter's Street for years. He'd learned advanced techniques and he was now able to work in all media—charcoal, pastels, and oils.

Now, with the war on, he was painting Gen. MacArthur and Gen. Eisenhower in oils, but he gave most of his artistic energy to Varga girls, with their long curvaceous legs, their ample bosoms, and their skimpy outfits. The artist Varga had created this familiar calendar girl, and many a soldier later had a Varga girl inside his locker as a pinup.

JUKEBOX SATURDAY NIGHT

When we went dancing, we usually went to Gennaro's on Metairie Road or to Lenfant's on Canal Boulevard, where we jitterbugged to the music of the jukebox. Sometimes we went to the Terrace Club on Downman Road, where Larry Veca's band played on Saturday nights.

A musician friend of mine told me that they used to get seven dollars a night per musician, and that was big pay in those days for an extra job. They were mostly all teenagers playing, but they were outstanding musicians, and they played in the Glenn Miller big-band style.

Then after dancing we stopped for a malt or a hamburger at Rockery Inn, where we sat in the car in a darkened lot and were served curb service. The loudspeaker played "Amapola" or "Green Eyes" or "The Bells of St. Cecilia." I will admit that this is the place where I learned the rudiments of kissing.

Al was the first boy I had ever kissed seriously. In fact, Al didn't even kiss me until our third date, and I wondered if there was something wrong with me. He later told me that he knew I was "a nice girl" and he didn't want to blow his chances.

A few other trial kisses had brushed my lips, all just good-night pecks. But I was in love with Al, and with him it was a whole new experience. Although it was just kissing, to a convent girl it was ecstacy and food for thought for the following week. I missed many a sociology lecture reliving the moments, as I gazed dreamily out the window of Marquette Hall and sighed.

On August 7, 1942, the marines landed on Guadalcanal in the Solomon Islands. The fighting was fierce, and it was not until February of 1943 that the island was won. In the Solomons, American troops learned the technique of amphibious warfare, involving land, sea, and air forces working as a team. Heavy rains made the jungle roads unusable, and troops waded knee-deep through thick, black mud. Malaria and other jungle diseases took their toll, and leeches and scorpions were everywhere.

FIRST DAY AT "REAL" SCHOOL— ACCELERATING AT LOYOLA

Fall came and with it the beginning of the real school year at Loyola. As I reached the top of the stairs of Marquette Hall the first day of school, a photographer stopped me and asked me to pose with two freshman boys for a picture for the yearbook. I was thrilled . . . until I found out that we were being photographed from the *back*, as we gazed in rapture at the Gothic spires of Holy Name Church. I still don't understand what his idea was in taking such a picture, but it appeared as a frontispiece in the yearbook of 1943.

In the registrar's office, my father's friend, Miss Discon, greeted me. "Well, Mary Lou, how nice that you're going to be attending Loyola!" Everyone acted as

Rockery Inn at 7039 Canal Boulevard, owned by John Signorelli, was a popular drive-in restaurant in the thirties and forties. People came from all over town to get the fried chicken. It closed in 1969 to make way for the Signorelli office building.

if summer school hadn't even happened. *This* was the real beginning. "Are you planning to accelerate?" she asked.

I had no idea what the word meant, but it sounded like "excel," so I said, smiling, "I'm going to try."

"Good for you!" she said, and took out the proper forms.

Loyola, like all other co-ed and all-male colleges all over the country, was now changing over to an accelerated program, meaning that the school would offer three semesters a year instead of two. This enabled boys to graduate in two years and eight months, thus speedily releasing them to the armed services. Girls were allowed to choose whether they cared to rush through college at such a pace. All of us did.

Audrey started Newcomb College that fall, but we still managed to see each other regularly. Vernon and I sometimes walked over to meet Audrey at the Tulane cafeteria for lunch. On other occasions, Audrey and her sister Betty, a senior at Newcomb, walked to the Loyola cafeteria. Audrey and I no longer rode the streetcars together daily, but we still slept over at each other's houses, usually on Friday nights.

Mass of the Holy Ghost in Holy Name Church kicked off the Loyola school year (September 1942). (Photo by Russ Cresson, courtesy Joan Garvey)

CITY-WIDE SCRAP
COLLECTION DRIVE

In September, the army staged a one-day drive for scrap steel and iron articles in the city. Mayor Maestri suspended garbage pickup that day so that the 250 vehicles of the department of public works could be used for metal collection. People were asked to put out their old stoves, toasters, lawn mowers, etc. Plowshares were indeed being beaten into swords, and pruning hooks into spears. Mother and I searched the house and came up with an old metal dress form for sewing that she hadn't used in years. She was reluctant to part with it, but in the end, we carried it out to the back street.

To the same end, the *Times-Picayune* newspaper announced a "School Metal Scrap Drive" in October. Picking this up, Jesuit High School issued a challenge to its traditional rival, Warren Easton High, to see which school could collect more metal. A picture in the *Times-Picayune* showed Al Widmer, Nicholas Stokes, William Schroll, Harold Breeding, and Rene Lazare as the challenging scrap committee. From Warren Easton came the reply, "We'll wipe 'em off the earth." And the fight was on.

The Jesuit plan was to have each student bring to school whatever scrap metal he could carry and give it to an appointed committeeman, along with a slip showing the address of his home where other scrap had been put out for collection. Trucks of parents and school neighbors were used in this daily scavenging, and the school yard soon became an immense scrap pile. One grocer in the neighborhood offered his old truck to help in the pickup and then donated the truck itself to the drive. The system worked so well that the Jesuit High team won, or so the committee claimed.

THE WINTER OF '42

As co-captain, Al led his football team to victory on the field at City Park Stadium every week, except for the final game with Warren Easton. It was the biggest high school game of the season and it was played at the Sugar Bowl Stadium at Tulane University. Jesuit lost that one and it broke Al's heart. This was his year, his tri-captain year, and winning City Championship meant more to him than life itself. It meant more to him than I did, and I knew that for a fact when we went to Gennaro's that night and he didn't talk, he didn't dance, and he didn't smile all evening. It had been a crushing blow. Al was an early Vince Lombardi. To him, winning wasn't the main thing. It was the only thing.

Christmas came around and Al gave me a red leather overnight case packed with Helena Rubenstein cosmetics, undoubtedly the most precious gift I had ever received. He had bought it with money saved from his job selling class rings. I used the makeup first and then the case for many years to come. Vernon and I had bought the boys wallets with oval silver ID tabs which we'd had engraved with their initials. The four of us exchanged gifts at Vernon's house beside her tree. It was a memorable evening, for we all knew our time together was growing short.

In June Al officially graduated, and in July of 1943 he was drafted. Within days, he left for boot camp in the marines at San Diego. After one furlough in September, he was sent to field communications school at Camp Pendleton, and since he was not to get another furlough when his course ended, we both knew

Pretty Loyola co-eds Hazel Holthaus and Betty Jane Haydel work in one of the city's many drives to collect scrap for the war effort.

he'd be going overseas. We wrote each other every day, repeating the same declarations of love and sadness at being separated. But we were to have one more week together before Al was sent to the Pacific. His mother and I took the Union Pacific to California to see him in January of 1944 at my semester break, and it was the last time I saw Al for two years.

The Rhythmettes perform in Loyola's Talent Night: May Glo Schilleci, Mildred Duffy, and Marie Lillo.

CHAPTER FIVE

The War Years: 1943–1944

EXCEPT FOR THE company of eight or nine girls, who have remained my lifetime friends, I don't know how I would have made it through the war years. Every weekend we did something together. We went to a movie or sunbathed at the lakefront in the summer months. Sometimes we had a slumber party, and we talked about our boyfriends and wrote letters and read them to each other. Then once in a while we got dressed up and went to Pat O'Brien's in the French Quarter to have a "Hurricane" and to join in the boisterous singing of college songs and war songs, while Mercedes and Sue, the nightclub's entertainers, beat them out on the double piano.

In July of 1943, Al sent me $200 with instructions to go to a jewelry store and pick out an engagement ring. He wanted to be able to say he was engaged, and since there was no other way to do it, he sent the money. I think we both wanted an umbilical cord that stretched across 10,000 miles, holding us together in a promise. Everything seemed so uncertain, so temporary, in those days.

Heart pounding, I selected a half-carat diamond in a gold tiffany setting, had my nails manicured, and showed the ring off to my friends in school the next day as if it were the Hope Diamond. The girls all hugged me and congratulated me. They gave me a Coke-and-cookie party in the Loyola cafeteria, and I was as happy as a lark. At last, I had a lasso around the man I loved, a long one that reached as far as the South Pacific. It wasn't like having him here, but it was second best.

Sunbathing at Lake Pontchartrain in 1943: Mary Joyce, author, Audrey, and Nellie.

LOYOLA'S RANKS WERE THINNING

By the spring trimester of 1944, the boys had almost all been drafted out of college or else they'd joined up. The only boys still on campus were seniors in dentistry or pharmacy, who were deferred until graduation, and a few 4-Fs (not qualified to serve).

55

GOOD LUCK, SOLDIER

Military greeting cards like this one helped us keep in touch with our loved ones in the service.

Now Loyola was taking all the girls who wanted to attend, just to keep its doors open. The Jesuit priests on the faculty had never taught girls before. Except for a few, they were easily duped by wily young women who made excuses for homework not done and begged them to postpone long assignments.

I think it is no exaggeration to say that we missed all the good things college usually offers. There were no yearbooks between 1943 and 1946 because of the shortage of paper. There were no student dances or fraternity dances, or even fraternities for that matter, because of the shortage of boys.

An air force unit had made arrangements with Loyola to use the fourth floor of Marquette Hall for classes, and we saw the servicemen filing into the cafeteria every day for lunch, all spit and polish in their uniforms. They did not carouse or flirt with the girls. Apparently they had been forewarned. So what good were they to us?

Servicemen sent home "Voice-O-Graphs" to tell the family news.

The USO on Carondelet Street, where servicemen relaxed. (Courtesy The Historic New Orleans Collection, Museum/Research Center, Acc. No. 1979.325.4080)

NELLIE, OUR CAMPUS QUEEN

In my first year at Loyola I had met a beautiful girl named Nellie, who had become a very close friend. She had one of the prettiest faces I've ever seen, and she was enormously popular, as long as there were boys around to be popular *with*. In the spring of 1944, she ran for and won the title of Campus Queen, an honor that the Blue Key organization had kept alive.

On the night of her presentation, the annual Talent Night program was to take place. Nellie was to give the winner a felt square with letters spelling out "First Place, Loyola Talent Night, 1944." My friends urged me to enter the contest, doing the impersonations I used to do just to entertain them: Katharine Hepburn in a scene from *Dragon Seed*, Bette Davis in *Watch on the Rhine*, Maria Ouspenskaya in *King's Row* (the movie in which Audrey and I fell in love with Ronald Reagan), and a few others that now escape my memory. Since there was nothing else interesting going on in school, I decided to enter.

To my vast surprise, I won, not because of my talent, but because no one else had the nerve to get up before the entire student body and make such an idiot of herself. It was something different from the usual piano accordion rendition of "Lady of Spain" and the soprano singing all six parts of the "Sextet from Lucia." The audience loved it.

It was especially memorable because my friend Nellie, the Campus Queen, handed me the trophy (the square of felt). But I have always regretted that there was no yearbook then. That would have been a full-page picture to show our grandchildren.

THE NICOLLETTES—AN ALL-GIRL BAND

Nellie's cousin, Marie Louise Nicoll, a music school student at Loyola (who is now deceased), put together an all-girl dance band made up of outstanding musicians she had known from Sacred Heart High School. They played for high school dances and parties. They were in great demand and could have played every weekend. Wearing matching evening dresses, they thrilled the crowds with dance tunes and specialty numbers. They earned three dollars apiece for a gig, which they spent immediately afterwards on food and drinks.

The Nicollettes, an all-girl band (average age, twenty), played during the war years for high school dances and parties: Dorris Murray, Mary Margaret Cusack, Genevieve Berry, Elaine Knap, Evelyn Kelly, Loretta Martina, Nellie Arnoult, Marie Louise Nicoll (leader), and Hazel Salles. Miriam Farina not pictured. (Courtesy Nellie Arnoult Schott)

Loyola Junior-Senior Prom at the Jung Roof.

Marie Louise played trumpet and Nellie played drums. When their pianist, Hazel Salles, left town to go live with her husband in the army, I took her place and played piano (badly). Then when Nellie and her mother went to New York, where her father was stationed, I filled in for her on drums (badly). But it was great fun, and it gave us a whole new interest to occupy our minds.

A WEDDING IN THE FAMILY

In September, Bob and Vernon were married, when my new baby sister Terry was only two months old. The bride and groom were both nineteen, young by today's standards, but so many were marrying young in the war years. Bob had found an apartment in Tyler, Texas, where several of the soldiers from Camp Fannin lived with their wives. Vernon made friends there with two young women with whom she corresponded for many years after returning home. One of the girls lost her husband in the war.

Vernon got a job as a dental assistant at Camp Fannin in Tyler. It wasn't what she'd been trained for, but the pay was good and she had to work. No couple could live on a private's pay.

In my senior year, I felt all alone, with Al and Bob and Vernon gone. I was practice-teaching at Wright High School, following in Vernon's footsteps, but Loyola seemed empty without its full complement of boys. The city seemed empty without its thousands of strong, capable young men, even if it was full to overflowing with lonesome, homesick boys in uniform from all other parts of the country.

Oil rig built in New Orleans at the Julia Street Wharf. The Hibernia Bank cupola towers twenty-three stories over the city.

CHAPTER SIX

The Home Front

AFTER THE INITIAL shock of Pearl Harbor, conditions of life in a country at war became known to us gradually. Each in itself was not a hardship to whine about, nor would anyone complain when our young men at the front were enduring so much worse. But as shortages became more serious and privileges more limited, as sorrows and griefs were shared, life gradually centered around one single issue. When would the war be over? When would our men come home? When would we resume our normal way of life, without fear that the next Western Union telegram would bring the unbearable message?

By 1944, the war had touched every phase of our lives. Stars on a background of silk hung in the windows of many homes, telling the world that a husband or son was somewhere far away in the service of his country. Women wore lapel pins with a star to give the same message.

Even those who had no sons or husbands or sweethearts in the fighting were affected. Patriotic signs ands mottoes were everywhere. A seven-story-high American flag hung outside Godchaux's Department Store on Canal Street, visible for blocks around. In shipyards, slogans painted on large signs read, "He who relaxes is helping the Axis." In banks, in the Telephone Company public office, in the Public Service office on Baronne Street, the most familiar sign, "Buy War Bonds," was displayed. By the end of the war, Americans had bought $49 billion in War Bonds.

In buses and streetcars, signs read, "We're all pulling together" and "Shoppers, take an early streetcar home; make room for the defense workers." In cartoons, artists had a field day with their own versions of "loose lips sink ships."

On radio shows, comedians closed with the admonition, "Bye-bye, buy bonds." Lucky Strike cigarettes advertised with the slogan, "Lucky Strike Green has Gone to War." (The dye used in making the cigarette packs green was needed for some war use, and the packages were thereafter, and forevermore, white.) Every program, every ad, every commercial, tried to get into the act.

(Courtesy Louisiana Power & Light)

New Orleans Public Service during the war. The display window shows "The Victory Rule." (Courtesy Louisiana Power & Light)

Going home from work during World War II. Sign at rear says, "We're All Pulling Together." (Courtesy Louisiana Power & Light)

May 20 was Armed Forces Day, to honor the military during the war.

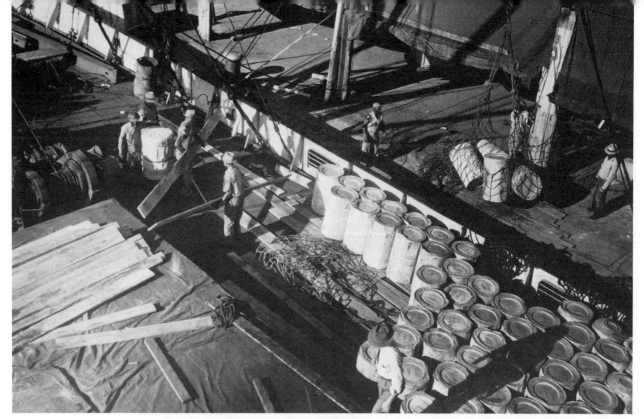

Loading a ship at Southern Railway's Chalmette pier, 1947.

The river at Canal Street with pedestrian ramps to Algiers Ferry. Note Poydras Street Wharf (lower left) and L&N Railroad shed (to right of ramp).

The Port of New Orleans, vital to the war effort.

NEW ORLEANS PORT, A VITAL CENTER

The task of keeping supply lines open for the fighting forces turned the New Orleans Port of Embarkation into one of the busiest and most vital shipping centers in the world. The tonnage handled through the port in 1944 increased by more than 300 percent over the previous year. The port was a vital center of the supply system for the global war. War materials of every nature, and ships as well, were loaded into the holds of waiting vessels and transports and sent to their destination without delay.

WARTIME AMUSEMENTS

At Pat O'Brien's, a popular nightclub in the French Quarter, and a "must" for servicemen passing through, the pianists Mercedes and Sue, at the double piano, had always been known for playing college fight songs and getting the customers to sing along with them. Now, with the war on, at least half their songs were war songs. They played "Praise the Lord and Pass the Ammunition" and the crowds went wild. They played "Remember Pearl Harbor," "You'd Be So Nice to Come Home To," "Boogie-Woogie Bugle Boy of Company B," "Don't Sit under the Apple Tree with Anyone Else but Me," "G.I. Jive," and "When the Lights Go on

Again All over the World." The locals and servicemen far from home sang along, sometimes laughing, sometimes crying, releasing emotions that were always close to the surface.

When Al came home on furlough, Vernon and I went to Pat O'Brien's with him, proud of him in his marine dress greens (Bob was then in Camp Fannin and he and Vernon were not yet married). When Bob came home on furlough, we went again. We listened to the rousing piano renditions and sang along and enjoyed a drink or two. Everyone had their pictures taken there in the war years, to keep a memory of those glad/sad times.

THE MOVIES WENT TO WAR

Movies of the period mirrored the hard-fought battles in Europe and the Pacific. The heroes were, of course, American servicemen. The villains were, of course, vicious Germans, Japanese with coke-bottle eye-glasses, and slow Italians. The plots were made to order. The American was taken prisoner and tortured to make him reveal some information—the location of his squadron, their plan of attack. The American held out until he fainted from the pain. In the end, he always triumphed, by virtue of his superior intelligence and patriotism. There were dozens of variations, based on prison camps, battles, campaigns, codes that were broken, spies, and women in the armed services.

Keep Your Powder Dry with Lana Turner was a story about women in the military. *Above Suspicion* with Fred MacMurray and Joan Crawford was about a honeymoon couple asked by the British to sneak Nazi plans for world conquest out of prewar Germany. *Five Graves to Cairo* with Erich von Stroheim was a reenactment of Rommel's African campaign. Von Stroheim gave an authentic rendition of the Hun you love to hate. And *Air Force* with John Garfield showed a Japanese Zero strafing an American parachuting to safety. War proved the adage that truth, especially truth embellished by the Hollywood scriptwriter, was stranger and more spellbinding than fiction.

Comic strips also reflected the war. Joe Palooka joined the army, giving his raincoat and his rations to a fellow dogface. Smilin' Jack became the gunner in the isolated nose of a bomber. Even Daddy Warbucks, in a general's uniform, made a deal by telephone with a German crew for their surrender, threatening to blow them to atoms if they refused.

CIVILIAN DEFENSE

Throughout the war, my father and thousands like him enforced blackouts during air-raid drills. A man on our block had volunteered for the Civilian Defense as a plane spotter. To do this, he had to study the lines and markings of enemy planes and stand regular hours watching the skies, ready to call headquarters if a suspicious plane was spotted. The fact that none ever appeared did not diminish the credit due such civilians.

High school boys, like those in the freshman class at Jesuit High School, made dozens of enemy planes out of balsa wood and painted them with authentic markings, to be used in classes for Civilian Defense plane spotters.

Ordinary civilians served on draft boards in every community throughout the country, making vital decisions as to whether or not young men were qualified to serve in the armed forces.

66

Displays encouraged careers in the military for women during the war.

WOMEN IN THE WAR EFFORT

Women were in every branch of the armed services during the war—the army (WAACs), the navy (WAVES, Women Accepted for Volunteer Emergency Service), and the air force (WAFs, Women's Air Force)—all performing administrative and technical duties to free men for combat. Women who flew Army Air Force service planes in other than combat duty were called WASPs (Women's Air Force Service Pilots). The last branch of women accepted in the military in World War II (February 1943) was the Women's Reserve Marine Corp, later part of the Regular Marine Corps (1948).

In training, it was discovered that WAVES could shoot even better than men, and not only rifles but the big hard-to-manage navy anti-aircraft guns. At the gunnery school at the Naval Training Center in Algiers, WAVES served as instructors. "On the whole, they are better shots than men," said Chief Petty Officer John W. Duffy, who was in charge of the gunnery school. "Some had never seen a gun before they enlisted, yet they make 'expert' in pistols. Then there's the mechanical part of it. These girls want to know everything about the

Author's friend Ruby Boudreaux (left) was in charge of the storeroom at Todd-Johnson, where equipment was kept to repair ships (1943). (Courtesy Ruby Boudreaux)

Ads for motorettes and conductorettes during the war. (Courtesy Louisiana Power & Light)

nomenclature and the breakdown of various types of guns, all of which makes them excellent instructors. Ordinarily, men might resent women training them, but our girls are so good, the men admire their ability."

Many female civilians were needed for defense work, since most of the productive male population was away from home. So women went to work in the shipyards. In New Orleans and its immediate vicinity, there were many defense plants and shipbuilders: Higgins, Delta, Todd-Johnson, Pendleton, and Consolidated Vultee Aircraft Corporation. "Rosie the Riveter" was more than just a cartoon character and the name of a song. She was reality.

Besides doing defense work, women were also working in many jobs formerly held only by men. They were now streetcar conductors and telephone linemen. They repaired radios, refrigerators, and other small appliances. They worked in offices, many in government offices. Women had joined the work force and they liked it. Their "place" would never be "in the home" again, unless they chose to make it so.

Late in 1944, my friend Audrey went into Nurses' Aide Training. The wartime program for aides trained them to take vital signs, bathe patients, make beds, serve lunches, and administer in many other ways to patients in hospitals all over town. The object of the program was to relieve registered nurses of their duties, so that they would be free to join the armed forces.

Audrey took her training at Touro Infirmary on weekends and after school. In January 1945, she received her cap at a candlelight ceremony, and began working with patients at Touro.

Author's friend Audrey as a nurse's aide in 1945. (Courtesy Audrey Villarrubia)

VICTORY GARDENS
AND SAVING CAMPAIGNS

By 1943, Victory gardens flourished in many backyards all over New Orleans. At the outset of the war, Secretary of Agriculture Wickard had surprised everyone by suggesting that since farmers would be busy feeding the army, civilians should plant Victory gardens to provide fresh vegetables for their own tables. In downtown New Orleans, on Iberville Street across from the Custom House, just a block away from the heavy traffic of Canal Street, a man named Harry Ducote planted a Victory garden on his parking lot. He was making the best use of it he could, since not many cars were "parking" during the war.

My mother began planting tomatoes, lettuce, beets, peas, and carrots in our backyard. She also learned how to can the excess for future use. Literature was available in reams from the Department of Agriculture and from seed companies giving advice on these procedures. Eventually, 40 percent of the country's vegetables were produced in Victory gardens in the nation's backyards.

Throughout the war, we also had dozens of "saving" campaigns. Everything we had formerly thrown away now seemed to have a wartime use. My grandmother turned in our old bacon grease to Mr. Herbert, our butcher on St. Peter Street, who then turned it over to collection volunteers. Old grease was used in making ammunition. Volunteers also gathered up tin cans, steel padlocks, and other metal to be used in the making of armaments. Old newspapers could be recycled into packing cartons for sending things overseas. Even old stockings were converted into powder bags. My little sister and brother saved our used-up toothpaste tubes for a drive at school, and felt that they were doing something patriotic.

Housewife "cans" vegetables from her Victory gardens during World War II.

EVERYTHING WAS RATIONED

And then there was rationing. Who would have believed that we could get along on only two pairs of shoes a year (and badly made shoes, at that)? We lived with our little ration books in our hands. Money was nothing if you didn't have ration stamps to go with it.

For food, this is how it worked. Meat, coffee, butter, cheese, sugar, and many other food items had specific point values, and the ration books issued to each family showed the point values of each stamp. Housewives paid the grocer with stamps as well as money. The grocer sent the stamps to his wholesaler to replenish his stock. The wholesaler turned in the stamps at his local bank and got credit to buy more food. During the war, grocers had to cope with some 14 billion points a month, actually handling about 3.5 billion ration stamps. In World War II, the black market boomed. Making counterfeit ration books became so profitable that the mobs took it over.

For the consumer, gasoline rationing was the biggest inconvenience. An "A" card—given to a doctor or a defense worker—allowed him three gallons of gasoline a week. All other drivers got two gallons. This resulted in the use of public transportation, car pooling, walking to work and school, and in many cases, gas-chiseling. But most patriotic citizens made do on their two gallons, *if* it was available.

New Orleanians stood in line for ration books—one line for shoe stamps, another for gasoline and tires. (Courtesy Library of Congress)

Wartime Shopping Guide

Item	Weight	Point Value
PORTERHOUSE STEAK	1 lb.	12
HAMBURGER	1 lb.	7
LOIN LAMB CHOPS	1 lb.	9
HAM	1 lb.	7
BUTTER	1 lb.	16
MARGARINE	1 lb.	4
CANNED SARDINES	1 lb.	12
CANNED MILK	1 lb.	1
AMERICAN CHEDDAR CHEESE	1 lb.	8
DRIED BEEF SLICES	1 lb.	16
PEACHES	16 oz. can	18
CARROTS	15 oz. can	6
PINEAPPLE JUICE	46 oz. can	22
BABY FOODS	4¼ oz. jar	1
FROZEN FRUIT JUICES	6 oz. can	1
TOMATO CATSUP	14 oz. bottle	15

Grocery shopping during the war. The sign on the freezer asks, "Please pay points and money at check stands." Lady with baby selects seed packets for her Victory garden.

A shopper complains about ration books as the grocer commiserates.

NEW ORLEANS
IN THE FORTIES

When motorists saw a gasoline tanker truck driving down the street, they formed a line following it to its destination. If you parked outside a theater, you could be turned in for joy-riding, and you'd have to forfeit your ration books. And if you needed new tires, you might just as well forget it. Get yourself some re-treads. The Japanese had seized the source of 90 percent of the world's rubber in the first three months of the war. Roosevelt had started a crash program for the creation of synthetics, but even when they became available, they all went to the war effort.

Travel was just about impossible. People would stand in line for hours for a train ticket. I didn't know how lucky we were to have made our trip to California when we did before things got really tight.

War ration books were complicated. Here is an example of instructions for use:

> All RED and BLUE stamps in War Ration Book 4 are worth 10 points each. RED and BLUE tokens are worth 1 point each. RED and BLUE tokens are used to make change for RED and BLUE stamps only when a purchase is made. IMPORTANT! Point Values of BROWN and GREEN stamps are not changed.

(Courtesy Walter and Josie Hogan)

My mother, for one, nearly went crazy trying to figure out the point system that regulated the purchase of food. And her grocer was of little help, since he was as bewildered as she.

During the war, it was patriotic to observe "Meatless Tuesdays," even if you had the stamps and the money to buy meat. It cut down on the demand for a scarce item and helped to stave off inflation. The Office of Price Administration (OPA) set the price ceilings on all goods, to avoid runaway prices in a time of shortages. The corner grocer read the lists that were sent to him and tried to label his goods according to government instructions, but it was not easy.

People began using oleomargarine as a substitute for butter, which was scarce, expensive, and required ration stamps. Oleo came in large plastic bags, looking like a slab of white lard, into which a yellow color ball had been dropped. Housewives sat at the kitchen table, breaking the color ball through the plastic package and massaging the color into the lard mass. No matter what we did to it, it still tasted like lard when spread on bread. But as time went on, the flavor improved, and by the end of the war, many households had been converted to oleo and never used butter again. Today it is generally called margarine.

Cigarettes were another scarce item. In college, everybody smoked. Cigarettes were sold a penny apiece, and you could buy as few as you liked. But it was not only Lucky Strike green that had gone to war, it was Lucky Strike itself, as well as Camels and Pall Malls and Philip Morris. The cafeterias, the grocery stores, and the drugstores were lucky if they had Wings and Picayunes to offer their customers.

Everyone groaned but they bought them. We all smoked like smokestacks and we had to have cigarettes if we had nothing else. Warnings about lung cancer had not yet been circulated, and all were convinced that in these trying times, cigarettes soothed our nerves.

A SOLDIER FOR SUNDAY DINNER

A wonderful act of kindness to servicemen away from home was to have them to Sunday dinner with the family. A white weatherboard building went up on Canal Street at Elks' Place where civilians could register by filling in a card, expressing their desire to have a soldier to Sunday dinner. Soldiers could also sign cards saying when they would be free to avail themselves of these invitations. Volunteers matched the soldier with the family.

Mother and I went there and signed a card, and within a week we were called. A Private First Class James Something—I forget his last name—from Houston, Texas, was in town for reassignment, and he'd accepted our invitation. He'd be at our house at noon on Sunday.

Private James Something turned out to be a slender young boy of no more than eighteen, obviously delighted to be in a home environment with a family. If nothing else, it beat standing in a chow line with a bunch of uniformed strangers.

"My son is stationed in Texas," my mother told the soldier, as she handed him his plate. "He's in Tyler. Have you ever been there?"

"Yes, ma'am," James answered with a broad Texas drawl. "I've got an aunt who lives there."

"Have you been to Camp Fannin? That's where he's stationed."

"No, ma'am, I sure haven't," he said sadly, as though he'd let us down, after how nice we'd been to him and all.

Veterans Service Center on Elks' Place and Canal Street after World War II. During the war, servicemen and local families were matched here so families could have a serviceman for Sunday dinner. Note the Romanesque Criminal Court behind. Southern Railway Station was just across Canal Street, to the right. (Courtesy The Historic New Orleans Collection, Museum/Research Center, Acc. No. 1979.325.5237)

We finally got him talking and helped him to relax. In the afternoon, we played cards and had cake and coffee and we even got to calling him Jimmy. Then my daddy drove him to Camp Leroy Johnson on the lakefront, where he was temporarily stationed.

We kept our names registered and had a soldier to Sunday dinner whenever we were called. It was almost like having Bob or Al to dinner, and we felt we were doing something for the men in uniform.

Audrey's Aunt Ella, a middle-aged single lady who lived with Audrey's family, used to pick up young servicemen two at a time on the street whenever she saw them and take them home for dinner. The young men soon found themselves sitting across the table from two pretty teenage girls, Audrey and her sister Betty, and undoubtedly went back and told their buddies how they had lucked out that day.

A friend of Aunt Ella's, another middle-aged single lady named Florence, sometimes saw a lonesome-looking boy in uniform and tucked her arm into his, saying, "Come on, chicken, Aunt Florence is going to treat you to a good meal at Galatoire's." And off they'd go, the young man not knowing what had happened until he'd tasted the restaurant's wonderful food and realized he'd been in the right place at the right time *that* day.

MILITARY INSTALLATIONS
ON THE LAKEFRONT

One area of the city that was transformed by the war was the five-mile stretch of recently reclaimed land along the lakefront. The only construction done during the war was that of military installations.

In the thirties, the lakefront had been transformed in anticipation of building five beautiful residential areas. A stepped concrete seawall, five and a half miles long, had been built on the floor of Lake Pontchartrain, approximately three thousand feet out from the shore. The enclosure had been filled with sand pumped from the lake bottom outside the seawall. Behind the seawall, the filled area had been raised five to ten feet above lake level, making it one of the highest areas of the city.

For this new waterfront, with its 2,000 acres of prime land, plans had been made for beaches, boulevards, parks, and a new municipal yacht harbor. But this was not to be—at least, not yet. Shushan Airport, now New Orleans Airport, built in 1934 on a man-made peninsula at a cost of $4.5 million, one of the biggest and best in the country, was at the eastern end of the five-mile reconstruction project.

Of the five residential subdivisions, only Lake Vista had been finished before the war, and only there had some houses been built before the shortages of material and labor stopped all construction. Lake Vista had been laid out in the "City Beautiful" design of Radburn, New Jersey, with a central "common," pedestrian lanes, and cul-de-sacs providing safe areas for children. Lake Vista is bounded by the lakefront and Robert E. Lee Boulevard, Bayou St. John and the London Avenue Canal.

In 1942, on the rest of the lakefront land, military installations began to mushroom. At the western end, near the lighthouse, was the Coast Guard Station. Moving eastward, in what are today West and East Lakeshore subdivisions, were the U.S. Army (Lagarde) General Hospital (west of Canal Boulevard) and the U.S. Naval Hospital (east of Canal Boulevard). For several years before the Naval Hospital was built, a drive-in theater was located on that corner of Canal Boulevard and Robert E. Lee.

Continuing eastward, on the lake edge of the Lake Vista subdivision, was a second Coast Guard Station after 1942. On the eastern bank of Bayou St. John, between Robert E. Lee and Lakeshore Drive, was a building housing the U.S. Maritime Commission.

Soldiers on obstacle course as they train at the Port of Embarkation during the war. (Photograph by U.S. Army)

The lakefront during World War II. Most military installations existed from 1942 until the end of the decade. (Map by Mary Lou Widmer)

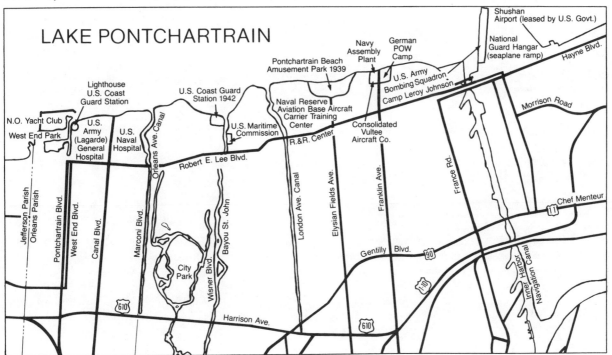

The Naval Reserve Aviation Base occupied an area on the lakefront between the London Avenue Canal and Franklin Avenue. Included in this area were an Aircraft Carrier Training Center and a Rest and Recreation Center. On Lakeshore Drive, on the western corner of Franklin Avenue was the Consolidated Vultee Aircraft Company, with its ramp which allowed seaplanes to be launched. A high chain-link fence prohibited vehicular traffic in that area along the lakefront.

Continuing eastward, between Franklin Avenue and Camp Leroy Johnson Road, stretched the barracks of Camp Leroy Johnson. Another interesting feature was the German POW Camp, on the far western corner of this area (Franklin Avenue and the lakefront).

Shushan Airport, at the end of Downman Road, was leased during the war by the U.S. government, and it housed a National Guard Hangar and ramp for launching seaplanes. Also, along its western wall was an area occupied by the U.S. Army Bombing Squadron. Pan American and Delta Airlines used the building jointly with the U.S. government for limited commercial activities. In 1947, Pan Am moved to Moisant Airport.

The lakefront had become the area for military installations, marking it the fringe of a mobilized city. All this was top secret, of course. Not until after the war was any information made available about these installations by the Levee Board, and pictures were never seen in newspapers or magazines anywhere, which is why they were so difficult to research.

U.S. Naval Reserve Training Center on Lakeshore Drive in the war years. It is still there today.

Michoud Defense Assembly Plant made planes before the war. It is shown here during World War II with dummy houses on the roof for camouflage.

FINANCIAL MATTERS

For the building of all these enormous projects, massive taxation was necessary. Income tax became virtually universal, and for the first time, taxes were withheld. Daddy and I looked at our paychecks, now reduced by the withholding tax, and felt depressed. We would have preferred to put it aside ourselves. It was the same, one way or the other, but somehow you felt as if you were making less money.

Then there was a graduated surtax ranging as high as 82 percent, and an across-the-board Victory Tax of 5 percent. But taxes paid only about 40 percent of the war costs. The national debt shot up from $43 billion to $269 billion by the end of the war.

At the same time, wages rose, and unemployment was wiped out, for the first time since the beginning of the Depression. We were happy about that, but somehow, higher wages didn't help. Prices were so high, you still seemed to spend everything you earned. To head off inflation, Roosevelt's agencies regulated wages and prices. They rationed or banned products to prevent a runaway market, they taxed heavily, and they encouraged savings.

Average civilians did not give in easily to all these controls. They resented the dictatorial powers of the president and his appointed boards, like the War Production Board, which had virtually unlimited powers since it was charged with the duty of transforming a reluctant civilian economy into a powerful war machine. Even with bombs falling, Roosevelt had a hard time pulling the many factions of the country together.

A photographer on busy Canal Street took candid shots of passers-by, then got their addresses to send prints.

CHAPTER SEVEN

Some of the Brave

2D LT. CHARLES ALBERT DONNELLY, JR.

CHARLIE DONNELLY ALWAYS loved planes. He made his first flight at four years old and told his dad, "Someday I'm going to fly a plane."

At Warren Easton High School, Charlie was a halfback on the football team. As a boxer, he won the A.A.U. Diamond Gloves 165-pound title. In 1942, he started at Tulane University, but was soon in the air force at Wichita Falls, Texas, pursuing his lifelong dream. After preflight, primary, and basic flight training, he was graduated as a fighter pilot. He won his wings and was commissioned as a second lieutenant on June 27, 1944.

After training for heavy bomber duty, he was sent overseas at the end of 1944. His actual combat service was brief, as he lost his life on his first mission. He was flying as copilot in a Liberator on December 20, 1944, to bomb oil refineries in Linz, Austria. The plane bombed its target in spite of one disabled engine, but on its return trip, two more engines failed, and the crew had to bail out near its home base on the Adriatic Sea.

Two crew members were rescued; eight perished by drowning. Charlie's body was found by Italian fishermen and buried with full military honors in Italy, to be returned, after the war, to New Orleans. He was awarded the Purple Heart, posthumously. Charlie was twenty years old.

STAFF SGT. JACK MAHAR,
U.S. ARMY AIR FORCE

Jack Mahar, a football player from Warren Easton High School, had by June 21, 1944, become Staff Sgt. Jack Mahar, a tail gunner of the Eighth Air Force. On that morning he left on his thirteenth mission, the first over Berlin. Just before reaching the target, his group was attacked by at least forty German planes. The American group downed about ten enemy planes, but three American planes were knocked out of formation.

The *Fortress* Jack was aboard was hit in the oxygen supply, located just behind the pilot and copilot. They were forced to leave the flight deck, allowing the plane to go into a tight spiral. The order to bail out was given, and when Jack managed to get his parachute on, he escaped through the tail gunner's hatch.

Landing near Berlin, the Americans were attacked and beaten unmercifully by German civilians, then taken prisoners by the German *Luftwaffe*. For eight months, Jack was a POW in Stalag Luft IV. He and his fellow prisoners were fed only once a day, with boiled barley. In February 1945, the Russians defeated the Nazis in a major offensive, and the Germans evacuated the prison camp. For three months, the evacuated prisoners were marched westward through Germany, going without food for sometimes three or four days. Sometimes they stole potatoes and salted pork from villages and farms, and cooked it on a stove they made from powdered-milk cans.

Their group was liberated just east of Luneburg by the English Second Army on May 2, 1945. Jack received the Air Medal, the Distinguished Flying Cross, and the POW Medal.

SGT. JAMES C. GULOTTA, TWENTY-FIRST RECON TROOP, INFANTRY DIVISION

James Gulotta, known as Jimmy to his friends on Sherwood Forest Drive, was a graduate of Alcée Fortier High School before his army days. On April 5, 1945, in Cebu, Philippine Islands, he volunteered to lead a small group accompanying four tanks to make a close-in reconnaissance of enemy positions. He chose this mission with the full knowledge that the tank group was intended to draw enemy fire in order to make them give away their strongest defensive positions.

As was expected, the enemy poured in heavy machine-gun and mortar fire, endangering Sgt. Gulotta and the men he led. At one time, the enemy attempted to flank the tanks and knock them out with demolitions. Sgt. Gulotta at once informed his section, then deployed his men, bringing such heavy fire on the enemy that the tanks were able to complete their mission and withdraw. Sgt. Gulotta's calm and quick action under fire and his sheer courage contributed materially to the success of the campaign.

In September 1945, several days after Japan's surrender, Sgt. Gulotta was among the officers and men who met the first Japanese surrender delegate on Cebu and escorted him to American Division headquarters. A Japanese lieutenant representing Lt. Gen. Kataoka, commander of the defunct Thirty-fifth Army, came through the lines at the Americans' invitation.

Sgt. Gulotta saw action on Guadalcanal, Bougainville, Leyte, and Cebu. He was awarded the Silver Star for gallantry in action.

LT. STANLEY F. ABELE,
U.S. NAVY FIGHTER PILOT

When Stanley F. Abele graduated from Samuel J. Peters High School in 1938 and then worked as a billing clerk for Crescent Cigar and Tobacco Company, he never dreamed that seven years later, he'd be a fighter pilot who would barely escape with his life. But that was what happened when his aircraft carrier, the USS *Bunker Hill*, was hit by two Japanese Kamikaze planes off Okinawa in 1945.

On May 11, 1945, at 10 A.M., Stan had just come on deck from the ready room, where his buddies were elated over the number of Japanese planes and ships they had hit on an earlier flight. The flight deck was jammed with bombers, torpedo planes, and fighter planes, loaded and ready for takeoff into battle.

Stan was about to get into his plane when the first Kamikaze clipped his upraised wings and crashed into the next four planes, killing all the pilots. The second followed and crashed into the bridge, after dropping a bomb which exploded in the hangar deck, killing all the men in the ready room. The flight deck was then a flaming holocaust.

Stan and other survivors made their way to a space above the fantail, where smoke and danger of ammunition explosion forced them to jump overboard. They were rescued by a destroyer and returned the following day to the *Bunker Hill*, which then set sail for Seattle for repairs. Of the crew, 392 were dead, 264 wounded. Lt. Stanley Abele, who flew forty to forty-five combat missions in the Pacific theater, received three Air Medals and a Distinguished Flying Cross.

PVT. WALLACE JOSEPH VILLARRUBIA, MARINE RAIDER

Wally Villarrubia, born in Lacombe, Louisiana, moved to New Orleans when he was ten. While attending Warren Easton High School, he worked out at weight lifting at the New Orleans Athletic Club. But his skill in paddling a canoe (paddling *into* the waves instead of around them to avoid capsizing) had been learned in his childhood in the bayous. This skill served him well when he was paddling rubber boats through New Hebrides and Guadalcanal, where he trained in the Fourth Marine Raider Battalion. His commander, Col. James Roosevelt, the president's son, always requested that Wally paddle his boat.

Wally had joined the marines on September 15, 1942, when he was twenty years old. After boot camp, he had a choice to make. He likes to tell the story that he always hated waiting in lines and since the line for the Marine Raiders was shortest, he got into that one.

On July 20, 1943, the First Raider Battalion and the Fourth Raider Battalion were trying to capture Bairoko Harbor, to gain control of Munda Air Field. As they approached through the jungle, Wally's buddy got hit. Wally crouched to assist him, and when he looked up, he saw a Japanese soldier aiming down at him. Before he could grab his rifle and shoot, the soldier shot him through the chest. The bullet hit a rib, ricocheted out and spun through his right elbow, shattering it. Wally had eight operations in the next eighteen months. He received the Purple Heart for being wounded in action.

TORPEDOMAN SECOND CLASS
ALLEN M. BORGES

Allen Borges, who had attended Warren Easton High School and LSU for one semester, enlisted in the navy early in 1943. A certificate hangs on the wall of his home, reminding him that he was among an elite group who were the first to set foot on Japanese soil on August 30, 1945, after the surrender of the Japanese Navy to the commanding officer of the USS *Piedmont.* The certificate reads:

> Be it known to all to whom these presents may come that Allen M. Borges, T.P. 2 C, USNR, as a member of the Tokyo Bay Occupation Force, participated in the initial landing in the occupation of the Tokyo Bay area and the capture of His Imperial Japanese Majesty's Ship *Nagato,* which act symbolized the unconditional and complete surrender of the Japanese Navy 30 August, 1945.

Allen says, "This certificate was given to everyone on the USS *Piedmont,* who were the first Americans into Tokyo Bay. The United States had dropped the first atomic bomb on Hiroshima on August 6, 1945, after which we were ordered to set a heading for Japan. Then on August 9, while we were underway, the second bomb was dropped on Nagasaki. Soon after, we entered Tokyo Bay to see what effect this had had on the Japanese military.

"The navy bowed to us as we entered, in a gesture of capitulation. Then on September 2, 1945, aboard the battleship USS *Missouri* in Tokyo Bay, the Allies and Japan signed the formal surrender agreement."

With a demolition squad, Allen remained in Japan till January, destroying the enemy's ammunition in the armory at Yokosuka by first neutralizing it and dumping it into deep water outside the bay. He and his crew received a Unit Citation.

PFC. SIDNEY HECKER

Sidney Hecker, a good friend of mine from Loyola University, should never have been in combat at all. He'd been rejected because of his eyesight when he'd tried to enlist. But he got his brother to pull some strings at the induction center and he was admitted into "limited" service at age eighteen. Nevertheless, after basic training, Sid found himself with a group of army replacements in the Twenty-eighth Infantry Division on his way overseas into the Battle of the Bulge.

"After ten days in a two-man foxhole under fire," Sid says, "we marched to a point near Clerveaux, Luxembourg, where a German panzer division came through, and we were forced to surrender.

"After walking five days and riding five more days in a boxcar, we were taken to a frame building, where we slept on tiered bunks made of branches, on straw mattresses with a single blanket. We were always cold. We had no toothbrushes, no razors. Our food was so repulsive, we refused to eat, then we *had* to eat, and we all got dysentery. There were no washstands or toilets. For 300 sick men, there was only a hole at one end of the cement floor of our building, Stalag IX B, that served as a latrine.

"I bathed only once in four months. Then when the snow melted in March, the mattresses and blankets became lice-infested. Our clothes and our hair were lice-infested. How any of us survived is a mystery. Many did not.

"We were liberated April 2, 1945, and I spent more time in the hospital than I had in the prison camp. I'd gone into combat at 165 pounds, and when liberated, I was 89 pounds."

Sid was discharged as a corporal and received the Combat Infantry Badge, three battle stars, and the POW Medal.

1ST LT. RODERIC G. MORERE

1st Lt. Roderic G. Morere, who grew up in Jefferson Parish, was called a "fighting fool and a wildcat" by his men. On November 3, 1943, his first day of combat duty with a rifle platoon, Lt. Morere, Company F, 180th Infantry Regiment, led his men in capturing his initial objective near Rocca Pipirozzi, Italy. He then led his platoon across an open field in pursuit of the enemy. When heavy artillery and mortar fire dispersed his platoon, Lt. Morere shouted to his men and encouraged them to follow him to a small knoll 300 yards away. A troop of enemy paratroopers, entrenched on the reverse slope, opened fire with machine guns. After crawling toward his objective, Morere, with accurate rifle fire, killed or wounded about thirty of the enemy.

The determined enemy attacked the platoon's position seven times, but by courageously moving about the platoon and skillfully directing fire, Morere helped his men repel each drive. Bullets penetrated his head and leg, but he crawled behind a rock and continued his accurate rifle fire and spirited leadership. Inspired by his heroic performance, his platoon held their ground and retained their objective. Morere was awarded the Distinguished Service Cross for extraordinary heroism.

On May 23, 1944, having recovered from his injuries, Lt. Morere took part in a drive which breached the Anzio beachhead encirclement. For gallantry and leadership, he was awarded the Silver Star Medal. He was also awarded the Purple Heart.

On August 11, 1944, his promotion to captain was announced. Roderic Morere died in 1988.

Roderic Morere.

Ralph Hogan.

STAFF SGT. RALPH F. HOGAN

Born on Zimple Street, Ralph Hogan was an uptown boy. After graduating from St. Aloysius High School in 1942, he worked at Consolidated Aircraft Corporation on the lakefront until he was drafted in 1943. Ralph became a gunner in the U.S. Army Air Force. He was on a mission to Berlin on April 7, 1945, when his B–17 was attacked by German planes. After shooting one enemy plane down, the B–17 was hit and fire forced the crew to bail out. After walking a mile, they were captured by German soldiers and taken to the mayor of the nearest town. They were interrogated and then accosted by the German pilot whose plane they'd shot down. He pulled his gun and seemed about to shoot them when the mayor calmed him down and sent him away.

They were taken to the town of Celle, imprisoned in a small jail for two days, and given only one meal. As Allied troops approached from the West, they were moved east to Uelzsen, and billeted in barnlike buildings with about five hundred other prisoners. Some had been there for five years; other were locked in shackles for offenses. After several days, those who were healthy enough were sent away from the oncoming Allies.

"During this march," Ralph says, "ten of us Americans and a Belgian got away from the others during an aerial attack and hid from our guards. We began moving westward, hoping to meet Allied troops. We were probably reported to authorities by local farmers, because we were recaptured later that evening and returned to Uelzsen. British forces attacked the town and fought for three days, while the prisoners had no food and little water. On April 21, 1945, the British took the town and we were free."

Staff Sergeant Hogan was awarded the Air Medal with two clusters, Battle Ribbons with two clusters, and a POW Medal.

Prisoner of War Medal. (Courtesy Ralph Hogan)

87

SGT. EDWARD L. DUPLANTIER, TANK COMMANDER

Eddie Duplantier, with his million-dollar smile, was one of my husband's dearest friends from his old Gentilly neighborhood. With Eddie, his cousin Leon, a few other "buddies," and their dates, Al and I spent many a Saturday night dancing at the Terrace Club on Downman Road before all the boys went into the service. After graduating from Holy Cross College, Eddie held several jobs before enlisting in the army.

At 9 A.M. on April 30, 1945, the last day of fighting in Munich, the last week of fighting in Europe, Eddie, twenty-one and then a tank commander in the Twentieth Armored Division, approached the Munich Airport. It was his third week of combat. He'd turned down a chance to go to Officers' Candidate School to get into the fighting before the war was over.

"We hit the airport pretty good," Eddie says. "Then my tank was hit with a German 88 shell, blowing a big piece of metal from the side of the tank across me like a guillotine and cutting off my legs. I started to get out through the turret, and my cannoneer pushed me up so that I was lying on top of the tank.

"I pulled myself off the tank because it was on fire, and when I fell, it was onto barbed wire, but I got out of that and dragged myself a few feet away. I was hit twice on the ground, and then I lay there all day, praying, until someone saw me move and sent the medics, who took me away in a jeep, all under fire."

In the next eighteen months, Eddie was in many hospitals until finally, in Temple, Texas, he got his legs. When he could walk with only one cane, he was discharged and sent home.

Eddie could have bled to death, but the doctors said that the difference in temperature between the white-hot metal that cut off his legs and the cold outside at the foot of the Alps caused his blood to coagulate. That saved his life.

He received a Purple Heart, a Bronze Star with a V for valor, and everyone in his outfit received a Presidential Unit Citation for that day.

CHAPTER EIGHT

Victory at Last!

IN MAY OF 1944, I received a letter from a marine named Malcolm Chatham. I frowned at the return address, not knowing the name, but I tore open the letter and read it. The writer told me he'd been a friend of Al's since they'd played football against each other when he was at Warren Easton High School. He said he'd run into Al overseas (I checked the letter; no inside address, no outside address except for Marine Administrative Command, c/o FPO, San Francisco). Al had then been in the Pacific theater for several months.

Malcolm told me that he had been on mess duty for four months, and when Al came through, he (Malcolm) had managed to get him a big juicy steak, and Al had really gone to town on it. Then he said that Al had left the island and gone on to "a new hunting ground." The hair prickled on the back of my neck when I read that. It sounded so ominous.

After the war, Al told me that they'd met in New Caledonia, which had already been secured, and that when he left there, he was going to Guadalcanal with a group of replacements. Guadalcanal had also been secured, so there was little to fear, but I didn't know that then.

Malcolm wrote this: "Don't worry, Lou. He's going to be all right. Nothing is going to happen to him. I've been here since January. I've seen friends from New Orleans come and go, and they make out all right."

His kind words made me cry. He had no way of knowing Al would be all right. Here I was reading a letter from someone who had just seen Al a few days before, and even so, I didn't really know if he was still alive. What a terrible strain to be under!

"I'm listening to music on the loudspeaker," Malcolm wrote. "They're playing, 'This Is a Lovely Way to Spend an Evening.' It makes me think of home, and it

At left: New Orleanians celebrate V-J Day and the end of World War II on August 15, 1945. (Photo by Oscar J. Valeton, courtesy Mrs. Yvonne Valeton)

makes me want to get this damned war over with." He signed it "Little Chatham" and below that, "Little Goon." Al later told me that everyone called his older brother "Big Goon" and Malcolm "Little Goon."

I answered Malcolm's letter and thanked him for trying to console me about Al's safety. Then a few months later, Al wrote me that he'd heard that Malcolm "Little Goon" Chatham had been killed in action on Guam. Al said he cried when he found out. And when he wrote me about it, I cried too.

In February 1945, I graduated from Loyola and began teaching school at Sacred Heart Academy on St. Charles Avenue. Father Coyle, my French teacher at Loyola, had sent me to Sacred Heart to coach some seniors after school, so they could pass French and graduate. The principal noticed my comings and goings, called Father Coyle to inquire about my grades and qualifications, and offered me a full-time teaching job beginning as soon as I graduated in February.

Actually, I started teaching *before* I graduated, when the new semester began at the end of January. I taught sixth, seventh, and eighth grade classes in English and social studies, and when I got my first check, I knew I was on my way to saving for my trousseau. I was earning $100 a month, $90 after taxes, but lunch was free, and they made a mean chocolate pudding in that cafeteria.

ROOSEVELT'S DEATH

In April of 1945, President Roosevelt died in Warm Springs, Georgia. He had suffered a stroke while having his portrait painted, exhausted by the massive burdens of the presidency and the war. From the Marianas Islands on Friday, April 13, 1945, Al wrote:

> We are all glued to the radio here listening to the news of the president's death. There are no words to tell how sad we are. I truly think he was the greatest president we've ever had. He's the only one I can remember in my lifetime. And to hear news like this when we're on the eve of victory takes the wind out of you and makes you want to cross your fingers about the future and the way this war will end. He was such a remarkable leader, and the world knew his strength. This is the time when we need him most. As for Truman, he'll have to prove his worth, but all we can say is that there is no one who can fill Roosevelt's shoes.

I read the letter and understood the fear and uncertainty of the men in the armed services.

But I didn't answer that letter. My sentiments on the subject were divided. I had grown up in a conservative Republican household. My father strongly disliked Roosevelt, and I had always been influenced by his opinions. It took more than a year or even a decade for me to arrive at an unbiased perspective of Roosevelt, but today, I sincerely believe that he was one of our great leaders.

On August 6 and August 9, 1945, the first atomic bombs ever used in wartime (called by the names Fat Man and Little Boy) were dropped on two Japanese cities, Hiroshima and Nagasaki. The Empire of Japan then surrendered. Al wrote:

> When we hear of the destruction and devastation that such a bomb can bring to the world, it's enough to put fear in the hearts of the hardest men. We can thank God we got it first and not our enemies. They say that using the bomb will save thousands of lives that would have been lost in the invasion of Japan, but I can't help but wonder if man might have gone a bit too far this time. In the hands of the wrong people, the atomic bomb could destroy the world.

A few days later, he wrote:

We stayed up till eleven o'clock Monday night [August 13], waiting for the news to break but it was not to come that night. It wasn't till Tuesday at four p.m. that we heard yelling and whooping coming from all sides. We all knew what it meant and we made a bee-line for the radio to hear the news. This is what we had been waiting for for such a long time. Japan had surrendered! The war was over! The celebration began.

Our C.O. had been stocking up on beer and when the announcement came over the radio that Japan had surrendered, he gave us a case of beer apiece, and in just a couple of hours, there wasn't a man among us sober. They just let us all go wild until we fell out for the night.

Audrey's sister Betty and her husband, Marine Air Corps Major Jack Dowd, in 1945.
(Courtesy Audrey Villarrubia)

NEW ORLEANS CELEBRATES

New Orleans went berserk. Whistles blew and the air-raid sirens screamed and for once, we knew we had nothing to fear, ever again. At home, we all kissed and embraced each other, thanking God that our boys had survived the long war and would soon be coming home to us.

94

We went out into the street, where we greeted neighbors and exchanged more hugs and kisses. On Canal Street, crowds gathered with people embracing total strangers and crying with joy. Some people in third- or fourth-floor offices dropped confetti on the milling throngs below. Ladies in their chapel veils and bandanas thronged into Jesuit Church to kneel in the pews and offer a heartfelt prayer of thanksgiving or light a votive candle.

When the day was over, I scanned my father's map in the hall. Colored pins marked many strange names like Siapan and Tinian and Tarawa and Iwo-Jima, places that had become quite real to our boys from New Orleans and Metairie and Kenner, many of whom had lost their lives or their limbs on that alien soil, many of whose bodies would not be brought home for burial for years.

I wrote Al that night that I felt a kind of peace I had not experienced in over two years, since I had last seen him. There would be months yet before he returned, since everything depended on the point system for discharge. Points were accumulated for time in service, time overseas, combat duty, etc. There were tens of thousands of men to be processed and brought home. It could not be done overnight, and it was only fair that those who had been gone longest or suffered most would come home first. But we could wait now. It was all over; there would be no more killing. Thank God for that.

The Weather
Fair, continued cool tonight, tomorrow.
High expected today, 72; low tonight 58.

LATE STOCKS PAGE 18

NEW ORLEANS ITEM

FINAL HOME

Sixty-Eighth Year—278   Monday, April 30, 1945   Price, Five Cents

WAR IN ITALY IS OVER

Mussolini Offered ★ ★ 'He Died Badly' ★ ★ Empire For His Life

Il Duce's body, lying in Milan Square, while partisans hold back the crowd.

Allies Mop Up 25 Nazi Divisions 'Torn To Pieces'

Rip Open Last Fort In Berlin

LONDON, (UP)—Red Army tanks broke into the Tiergarten, fortified core of the last eight-square-mile pocket of resistance in Berlin, and both the Russians and Nazis said the climax of the battle was at hand today.

A Moscow dispatch forecast that Marshal Stalin will have his greatest symbolic victory of the war—the capture of Berlin—to present to the Russian people for their May Day celebration.

"This is the climax in the battle of Berlin," a United Press correspondent reported from Moscow. "While the Moscow garrison parades before Marshal Stalin in Red Square tomorrow, it is very probable that his Berlin armies will overrun the last fanatical holdouts.

TANKS IN TIERGARTEN

ROME, (UP)

ROME, (UP)—Allied victory in Italy was announced today by Gen. Mark W. Clark in a triumphant proclamation that 25 German divisions had been "torn to pieces" and no longer could resist effectively the U. S. Fifth and British Eighth Armies.

"The military power of Germany in Italy has practically ceased," Clark said. His statement put the official seal on clearest evidence that Nazi resistance in north Italy was collapsing.

The Allied commander in Italy issued his victory announcement as his Fifth and Eighth armies were stampeding the high north Italy. The British captured Venice. Jugoslavian forces were reported fighting in the streets of Trieste toward which the British Big 8th Army was driving only 58 miles away. The Americans took Alexandria in northwest Italy and the British took Chioggia in the northeast on the Adriatic Sea.

END OF TRAIL

The Allies had come to the trail's end in the push up the Italian boot. It began at the Reggio di Calabria toe of the boot when the Eighth army stepped across the strait.

120,000 CAPTURED

9th Army Links With Russians

PARIS, (UP)—American and Russian troops effected a second juncture on the Elbe River today, broadening the Allied wedge between Germany's collapsing northern and southern front.

The new link up on the Elbe came as the Nazis' vaunted Bavarian redoubt in the south broke wide open under converging blows by five and perhaps six Allied armies storming in on the mountain stronghold from all sides.

'Frisco Parley Races Against Nazi Collapse

By Lyle C. Wilson

SAN FRANCISCO, (UP)—United Nations delegates began speed-up program today under the pressure of fear that the conference will begin to disintegrate the moment German resistance ends.

Il Duce Lies In Dishonor

BY JAMES E. ROPER

MILAN, (UP)—The battered, begrimed body of Benito Mussolini lay today in a Milan square—on a plot of dirt in a heap with 17 other corpses.

"HE DIED BADLY"

"Mussolini died badly," said Edoardo, leader of the 16-man firing squad which sent the dictator to his death.

Jahncke Sc Monopoly Suit Against AFL

Officials of Jahncke Service, Inc., are contemplating "appropriate court action" against the American Federation of Labor as a result of recent "monopolistic control" of all building and construction projects in the New Orleans area, a spokesman for Jancke said today.

FIRM REJECTS CONTRACT

Juveniles

In Memphis Have 'Mother Confessor' Who Knows Their Problem And Her Law

The Juvenile Court of New Orleans has figured in recent news headlines. To acquaint Orleanians with procedures in other Juvenile Courts, The Item today prints the story of Judge Camille Kelley of Memphis.

MEMPHIS, Tenn.—They call her "Dixie's Mother Confessor" and in all her 25 years on the bench of Memphis' Juvenile Court where she has tried the cases of nearly 50,000 errant boys and girls, Judge Camille Kelley, the South's first and most noted woman jurist, has lived up to that appellation.

HER METHOD WORKS

"GREATEST SOCIAL ARENA"

NEW ORLEANS STATES

EXTRA

VOL. 65—NO. 107   New Orleans, La., Monday, May 7, 1945   PRICE CITY AND COUNTRY 5c

GERMANY SURRENDERS

AMERICAN TANKS DRIVE THROUGH THE TRAIL OF RUINS THAT ONCE WAS GERMANY

Reims, France, May 7.—Germany surrendered unconditionally to the Western Allies and Russia at 2:41 a. m., French Time today.

(This was at 8:41 p. m., Eastern War Time Sunday.)

The surrender took place at a little red schoolhouse which is headquarters of General Eisenhower.

The surrender which brought the war in Europe to a formal end after five years, eight months and six days of bloodshed and destruction was signed for Germany by Colonel General Gustav-Jodl.

Jodl is the new chief of staff of the German army.

It was signed for the supreme Allied command by Lieutenant General Walter Bedell Smith, chief of staff for General Eisenhower.

It was also signed by General Ivan Susloparoff for Russia and by General Francois Sevez for France.

THE "BIG THREE" AT TEHERAN IN 1944 AS THEY PLANNED TODAY'S VICTORY

CHAPTER NINE

1945—The Biggest News Year in Our History

On February 4, 1945, the "Big Three"—Roosevelt, Churchill, and Stalin—met at Yalta on the Black Sea to agree on plans to occupy Germany, set up a new Polish government, and form a United Nations organization. At this meeting, Russia promised to declare war against Japan three months after Germany surrendered. For this, Russia was promised the Kuril Islands and the southern part of Sakhalin Island, which Japan then controlled.

No one knew then, however, that Russia would not keep her promise, but would wait until after the atomic bomb had been dropped to come into the war against Japan. And that when Russia did come into the war, it would also seize Manchuria and North Korea, setting the stage for the Korean War. Another promise Russia did not keep was to allow free elections in Poland. Stalin used the Yalta agreements to enslave millions of people.

There was much political controversy over this meeting in the United States. Some said that Roosevelt sold us out at Yalta, others that he had trusted Stalin too much. In any event, two months later, a sick and war-weary Roosevelt was dead.

In the year 1945, one kind of world ended and another began. It was the biggest news year in the history of our country . . . until 1989. In 1945, the greatest war in history ended. Roosevelt died. Mussolini died. Hitler committed suicide. Churchill was voted out of office. The United Nations was founded. The republic of Vietnam was established with Ho Chi Minh as president. The first atom bomb was dropped, the German death camps were revealed, and mankind wept at the proof of its own capacity for evil.

The Nuremberg trials documented the extermination of ten million people, factory style. In his fanatical obsession with removing Jews from Europe, Hitler had sent approximately six million Jews to their death. They had been shot, beaten, starved, buried alive, and in the end, sent in a systematic fashion to the gas chambers.

On August 6, 1945, a B–29 called the *Enola Gay* dropped the first atomic bomb used in warfare on the city of Hiroshima, Japan, obliterating 4.7 square miles of territory. A few days later, on August 9, another atomic bomb wiped out 1.8 square miles of the city of Nagasaki. More than 100,000 persons were killed, and 110,000 injured.

On August 14, the Allies received a message from Japan, accepting the terms of surrender. On September 2, aboard the battleship *Missouri,* the Allies and Japan signed the surrender agreement. President Truman proclaimed September 2 "V-J Day" (Victory in Japan). Three years, eight months, and twenty-two days after Pearl Harbor, the United States was once again at peace. World War II had ended.

Whether the use of the atomic bomb on Hiroshima and Nagasaki was necessary will never be determined to everyone's satisfaction. In the planned invasion of Japan, it is estimated that there would have been a half-million American casualties and many times more that number of Japanese. The bomb seemed necessary at the time. It was dropped, and the war ended. In later years, President Truman was often quoted as saying, "I don't apologize for the bomb. I'm still waiting for Japan to apologize for Pearl Harbor."

At the war's end, the United States had become the undisputed leader and the greatest power in the world. Great Britain's time had passed. Germany and Japan had been bitterly defeated. Churchill told Parliament in the summer of 1945, "America at this moment stands at the summit of the world." For four years, until the Russians exploded their own atomic bomb, the United States was without equal in the world.

MY OWN "BIG NEWS" YEAR

Like so many other young women who waited for their men to come home from the war, I found 1945 to be my own year of red-letter events. In February 1945, I graduated from Loyola and started teaching school. On August 15, 1945, I heard the news of the Japanese surrender on the radio and rejoiced with my family and friends, knowing that it was all over and Al would soon be home. In December 1945, Al arrived in California, four months after the surrender of Japan.

He wrote that he needed forty-five points for discharge and he had only forty-four. He was sent to a Reclassification and Relocation Center in San Diego, where men without enough points for discharge were given further orders and sent on furlough. He said he'd be home, but not discharged, on a thirty-day furlough by December 10.

That was all I needed to know. We had planned to be married as soon as he got home. Al was twenty-one and I was nineteen and we'd been in love for four years. He was coming home with $1,000 in savings, a fortune in those days, especially to young people who had grown up during the Depression. He would be going to college on the new G.I. Bill, which would pay all his expenses, including books and a cost-of-living check of $90 a month. With my salary of $90, we would be almost wealthy. Our parents approved of the wedding, so there was nothing to hold us back.

For months, I had been making plans, whatever plans *could* be made. I had selected china and crystal patterns. Silver was not to be found. I had bought a dress pattern and the white slipper satin for my wedding gown and turned it over to my dressmaker, Mrs. Scott. I had been buying a few sheets and towels each month for my cedar chest. Now I was ready to buy the material and patterns for dresses for my bridesmaids: my sister Elaine, my sister-in-law Vernon, and my best friends Audrey and Nellie. I also went shopping for a "going-away" suit and overcoat, a hat, bag, gloves, shoes, and a few trousseau dresses.

With the December 10 homecoming in sight, I set the wedding date for December 29. I reserved St. Anthony's Church for eleven o'clock Mass on that Saturday morning, and made arrangements with my parents to have the reception at home. Neither they nor Al had money enough to rent a hall. I had invitations printed, addressed them, drew in a deep breath, and dropped them in the mailbox.

Banns were announced for three consecutive Sundays in church, and Audrey and Vernon both gave me bridal showers. Fittings were underway for my dress and the bridesmaids' dresses. But by December 15, there was still no Al. He called me each night, explaining some new delay, some red tape that was keeping him in San Diego.

One day when I was shopping on Canal Street, I met Joy Gomes, Audrey's friend from Newcomb. "Is Al home yet?" she asked.

"Not yet."

"Oh, my God!" she exclaimed. "Aren't you worried sick that he won't get here in time for the wedding, with your invitations in the mail and everything?"

I laughed off her question, but inside, I suddenly panicked. Suppose he didn't make it home on time. What if they cancelled his furlough?

Suppose, I thought, as I lay wide-eyed in bed that night, just suppose . . . we found out we weren't still in love after all this time. Suppose the love letters we'd been writing for two years had just become routine, like a daily report to an imaginary person you no longer remember. Suppose when he came home, I found out that the *real* Al was a stranger to me, someone I didn't really want for a life partner. Or suppose *he* discovered that about *me*. I sat up in bed, heart racing, wondering if we were doing the right thing, making such irrevocable plans, when we really didn't know each other at all.

Al's Aunt Jane hadn't helped the situation by saying she'd heard that men coming back after a long stay in the jungles of the South Pacific didn't know how to get in and out of a bathtub anymore, that they needed help. She said they had to be taught all over again how to use a knife and fork. Of course, I know now she didn't want us to get married so young and she would have said anything to keep us from doing so, but I didn't know that then. When I told Al this story on our honeymoon, he threw back his head and laughed.

"Where in the Hell does she think we were, on another planet?" he asked. "How can a grown man forget how to get in a bathtub, unless he's had a frontal lobotomy or something? My God, Lou, how could you listen to that kind of drivel?"

I had to laugh at myself then, and the laughter was a catharsis. At the time Aunt Jane had said all that, it had been so long since I'd seen Al that I would have believed almost anything.

But back to San Diego. In his last week before furlough, Al was interviewed, he heard lectures about the G.I. Bill and other veterans' rights, and he wrote me

Union Station. (Courtesy The Historic New Orleans Collection, Museum/Research Center, Acc. No. 1979.329.6096)

letters, assuring me that he'd be home for the wedding, even if he wasn't discharged. He'd have a whole month in New Orleans, plenty enough time for a honeymoon. Then he'd undoubtedly have to go to Camp LeJeune, North Carolina, to wait on that last point to be discharged.

He came home on the 20th, and his mother and aunts and cousins and I met him at Union Station. I ran to him first and we hugged and kissed and cried, and I couldn't believe I was looking into those green eyes. I resented giving him up even for a second for him to kiss his mother and greet his family. He was mine now, and we were going to make it official in just nine days.

Wedding presents arrived each day, and what a thrill it was to have him with me when I opened them! It seems we spent that whole week before the wedding visiting relatives and attending parties given by friends. But at last the day arrived.

Checking myself out in my dresser mirror, I smiled. I was delighted with my slipper satin gown with the white marquisette yoke and the long narrow sleeves ending in a point over the wrist. I loved the fingertip veil held secure by a tiny crown of orange blossoms and seed pearls. And I loved the fragrance of the gardenia cascade I was holding. Gardenias had always meant proms and corsages and weddings.

Author on wedding day with husband, Cpl. Albert Widmer, December 1945. The "swirls" hairdo marks the forties.

The limousine arrived at the duplex on the Orleans Canal. Daddy, proud as a peacock, helped me in and then sat beside me, preening.

The wedding was lovely, with the church still decorated for the Christmas season. All my bridesmaids were beauties, not one over twenty-one, not one over 110 pounds. It was more like a style show or a fashion parade, except that they were all dressed alike. And Al's pretty little cousin Deanna was our flower girl.

The reception at my family home was beautiful. I enjoyed the good wishes of family and friends, and the wonderful refreshments, but I didn't let go of Al's arm for a second. In the afternoon, we left on the L&N train at the riverfront for the Markham Hotel in Gulfport (now gone). It was not my first choice, but it was all we could get, what with the football crowds descending upon the city and the Gulf Coast for the Sugar Bowl game.

The east end of the cavernous L&N trainshed at the New Orleans depot (Canal Street and the river). This railroad took us to the Gulf Coast for our honeymoon in 1945. Movie buffs saw this station immortalized in A Streetcar Named Desire. *(Photo from the collection of Harold K. Vollrath, courtesy Old Kenner Railroad Association)*

A COACH'S DREAM: FIVE YEARS OF ATHLETES TO CHOOSE FROM

As soon as we returned, even before he left for Camp LeJeune to get his discharge, Al made inquiries at Tulane about playing football there. Before joining the marines, he'd been promised a football scholarship on his return by "Little" Monk Simon, who'd been the Tulane Coach before the war. But Monk Simon was no longer there. He'd been replaced by Henry Frnka, who was not a New Orleans man and knew nothing about Al Widmer and his tri-captain status at Jesuit. What was more, Frnka had five years of athletes, all outstanding, all high school graduates, trying to get on the squad. What a lineup of talent to choose from!

He told Al what he'd told all the others. "Come out for spring practice, and we'll see how the team shapes up." It was the only fair way to proceed.

Of course, Al wasn't looking for a scholarship. Uncle Sam was going to pay his way through college. But all along, he had hoped to play college football and he had to give it a try.

With nothing definite decided, Al left for Camp LeJeune in January 1946, with six weeks left to serve before he would be eligible for discharge. That was too long a time for him to make the February 18 registration. And if he missed the spring semester, he'd have to wait until fall to go to college. But his commanding officer in North Carolina took pity on his situation, and quickly granted him his last point. He arrived in the early morning hours and tapped at the side door. I opened the door for him, and we clung to each other, never to be separated again.

In February, Al started at Tulane. In March, he tried out for the football team. But after a month of brutal daily scrimmages, followed by several hours of studying for his classes, Al decided to quit football and transfer to Loyola. And so Loyola became his alma mater too.

Higgins Industrial Canal plant, builder of wartime landing craft and PT boats, converted to the manufacture of cargo vessels, yachts, and pleasure craft after 1945.

CHAPTER TEN

The Aftermath of War

A CARTOON IN THE *Times-Picayune* late in 1945 showed a blacksmith with a mallet and tongs trying to beat the swords he'd made back into plowshares. America was converting to peacetime. But questions arose, for there was no precedent to conversion on such a massive scale. How does a country change huge defense plants into (or *back* into) factories for peacetime production? Who pays the costs? And how long does it take? Americans were earning good salaries now, and people had been deprived too long. They wanted merchandise to buy and they were eagerly awaiting its arrival.

A TIME OF NEW FEARS

Somehow we couldn't let go of the war. It had a paralyzing grip on us. Newspapers carried stories of Hitler's death in every issue. At parties and gatherings, we all speculated—had Hitler really died with his bride of thirty-six hours in a bunker under the bomb-blasted Reichschancellory? Or had he escaped to show up somewhere else in the world after a period of hiding?

Fear of the return of the man responsible for the world's most costly war and the loss of fifty million lives lingered for decades. It was still a subject of conversation in 1978, when the movie *The Boys from Brazil* was made with Gregory Peck. But my father assured me that the British had the story from Germans who had been with Hitler the last few hours of his life. They swore that Hitler had married Eva Braun, the two had committed suicide on April 30, and their bodies had been burned.

But there were other fears stemming from the war and they fell, more or less, into two categories. One, how would the atom bomb affect the future of the world? And two, what threat to world peace did Russia now pose?

Anxiously, we read the accounts of the deaths and mutilation of 200,000 people and the obliteration of entire sections of the two Japanese cities. What if Russian scientists worked out the formula for the atom bomb? Radioactivity was a new concept, an unknown force, and a subject of intense interest. It was being used with great care in experiments on animals. Scientists were using Geiger counters to detect its whereabouts. The first atomic rocket was shot off in 1946.

Our fear of Russia was one of long standing. We had been allies during the war, but wary and uncomfortable allies. Russia's treachery had already been demonstrated when she'd violated the Yalta Agreement, the first agreement made with the United States, thus setting the pattern for the "cold war" and for our later involvement in the Korean and Vietnam wars.

Fear of Russia produced a general fear of communism. J. Edgar Hoover spoke of Communists living here in the United States who had allegiance to Russia. "We must take steps to immunize them," he said, "so they can do no harm."

STRIKES IN THE MAJOR INDUSTRIES

For the present, the nation's main concern was with industry. Steelworkers struck for higher wages to meet the ever-rising cost of living. President Truman tried to mediate without success. Strikes also broke out in the Railroad unions, threatening to paralyze the economy of the nation. Picket lines were becoming a common sight.

I had a personal interest in the Telephone Company strike in the spring of 1947. I was working there at the time, and it was a new and terrifying experience for those of us who crossed the picket lines.

After a year and a half of teaching, I was convinced that I was too young to command discipline in the classroom. A change of jobs was mandatory. My sister-in-law Vernon had started working at the Telephone Company before I did, and she liked the work. She was a service representative in the business office, taking orders for installations, cancellations, transfers of service, and general complaints. In 1946, I followed her there, and in my wake came several other friends from Loyola and Newcomb. The Telephone Company was hiring college graduates who would hopefully stay with them a while and work toward executive positions.

I was hired at a salary of $125 a month, a substantial increase over what I'd earned as a teacher. The Telephone Company put me through a six-week training program with full pay, and I was delighted with my working conditions. As long as Al was in college, I had to work, and I couldn't think of any place I preferred to be.

While we waited for our training to begin, we took incoming calls from people applying for new telephone service in a temporary office named the "Calling Bureau." Facilities were not available for the thousands of new families branching out in new neighborhoods all over town. So we answered the telephones ringing all day and gave each caller the same pat spiel:

> "Ordinarily, we would be happy to furnish you with service, but at this time, facilities are not available. However, we are hard at work to provide them. If you would like to leave your name and address . . . "

And months later, when these customers *did* get service, they got two-party or four-party lines. Only a doctor or someone on emergency call got a "straight" line. And oh, what party-line complaints we had to handle after that!

In the spring of 1947, Vernon and I were asked to join the union. The minute we declined the invitation, union members who had formerly been our friends became our enemies. After a few weeks of snide comments and cold shoulders, we learned that a strike for an increase in wages was scheduled to begin shortly, unless the union demands were met. Through the grapevine, we learned that out of about two hundred service reps, only thirteen or fourteen were planning to cross the picket lines. We were scared to death. We agreed that our small group would meet at Walgreen's drugstore on Canal and Baronne at eight o'clock the first day of the strike and walk together to the Telephone Company business office.

From a half-block away, we could see the picket lines and the union workers milling around the entrance, waiting for the strike-breakers to cross through. Our knees began to tremble, but we marched on, holding hands, forming a kind of phalanx. As we neared the building, we saw union officials writing our names down in notebooks. What were they planning to do to us? A few of the girls got "egged," but we made it into the building and sighed with relief.

The first day was a scene of total confusion. The managers had not known how many service reps would show up or where they would be most needed. So they sent us to replace the cashiers taking phone bill payments, or to work in the cafeteria or in the elevators. Our regular jobs were forgotten.

By the second day, the managers had us better organized, and we were given more vital jobs. Some of us were put in cabs and sent to the Walnut Central Office, still a manual office, where dial phones had not yet been installed. There we called the numbers requested by the Walnut customers, but only emergency calls were put through.

In the days that followed, we learned to be Intercept Operators, Trouble-shooter Operators, and even Long Distance Operators. We were acquiring a broad overview of telephone company procedures we would never have learned otherwise, valuable skills that would help us in our own jobs when the strike was over. We worked hard, sometimes fourteen hours a day, but we laughed a lot and we came away with some memorable stories. All went well until the union sent some state officials to enforce a Women's Labor Law limiting the number of hours women could work in a day. We kept on working, but on a 9 to 5 schedule.

The weather was already hot, I remember that. Huge oscillating fans had been placed in strategic locations in the aisles of the operators' floors. The windows were all open wide, allowing the aroma of roasting coffee from nearby coffee companies in Faubourg St. Mary to waft into the huge fifth-story rooms.

The strike lasted six weeks, and the strikers got their raise. But the bitterness between union and non-union workers lingered for many months after it was over. The pleasant relations we had so enjoyed before the strike were lost for a very long time.

UNEMPLOYMENT, SHORTAGES, AND THE BABY BOOM

While some veterans went to college on the G.I. Bill and others were lucky enough to find jobs, there was a third class of ex-G.I.s, numbering in the thousands, who were unemployed. The government had agreed to give them unemployment pay of $20 a week for 52 weeks, so many decided to take it easy for a year after the war. The 52–20 Club, they were called. They jammed the unemployment offices once a week to get their checks, and resentment built against them among conscientious, hardworking veterans. Except for two friends who had graduated in dentistry, all the boys in our crowd were back at Loyola or just beginning Loyola on the G.I. Bill. Multiply my little group of friends by

Social functions got back to normal once the young men returned from war. Here is the U.B.L. Fraternity's Sweetheart Formal of 1947, at Loyola: Rosario Schilleci, Ann Duffy, Joe Bassetta, Mildred Duffy, U.B.L. "Sweetheart" Joan Springmann, Jimmy Di Leo, Bob Grisoli, and May Glo Schilleci. (Courtesy May Glo Monteleone)

After the war (1947), students chat before zoology class in Bobet Hall at Loyola. Note girls in bandanas, one wrapped around the head like a tignon. Boys dressed this way for class. (Courtesy Joan Garvey)

thousands all over the country, and you can easily understand why houses to rent were at a premium.

Construction had been at a standstill for four years. Now, suddenly, thousands of new families were looking for a place to live. If someone told you about an apartment to rent, you dropped everything, left work, and took a taxi in the hope of getting there in time to beat the dozens of others who were surely on their way. The problem was gargantuan. It was a boon to only one group of people, the construction workers, who had been promised lumber and other scarce building materials in a short time.

After searching all over town, Al and I decided we had no choice but to remain living with my family. There we stayed for seven years until Al was out of college and we had finally made our last payment on a lot in Lakeview and built a small brick house. That was in 1953.

In the late forties, the mayor asked the commission council to agree to a proposal made by the Parkview Gardens Company for building 421 homes in the area bounded by Mirabeau, Paris, Filmore, and Cartier. Each house would sell for $12,000. A second project was proposed by R. E. E. deMontluzin for building 90 three-bedroom houses on Virgil Boulevard between Gentilly Road and Paris Avenue. These were also to sell at about $12,000 a house.

Residential construction begins in the late forties.

deMontluzin asked that the city cooperate by building a bridge across the London Avenue Canal at Virgil Boulevard. These same builders had completed a 152-unit subdivision known as Maple Ridge Park in Jefferson Parish between Metairie Road and Airline Highway. Solving the housing shortage was a hot subject.

Though many of us lived with our families, and many of our husbands were still in school, babies made their appearance all the same. In the years between 1946 and 1950, many of my friends had one or two children. Thirty million war babies were born between 1942 and 1950. Before 1950, we were regularly attending baby birthday parties, complete with a carousel on the back of a truck or a clown scaring the life out of all the beautifully dressed little toddlers. A whole new generation of children was being born of veteran fathers, children who would face another war some twenty years later in Vietnam.

London Avenue Railroad Bridge and underpass in 1949, built under the Morrison administration. (Courtesy The Historic New Orleans Collection, Museum/Research Center, Acc. No. 1988.31.146)

Postwar building behind the French Market.

Postwar construction near the riverfront and warehouses.

HERE AND THERE IN THE CITY

New Orleans was still a small town in 1946. Only about half a million people lived in the metropolitan area. Things still moved at a much slower pace here than in Northern cities and our life-style was much simpler.

The area around *Lafayette Square* had its daily quota of bums and drunks. In *Uptown New Orleans,* there were lots of chinaball trees, which made a mess when the balls fell and pedestrians squashed them underfoot. There were also thousands of caterpillars in the spring in the giant oaks lining St. Charles Avenue. I remember that, because when I taught school at Sacred Heart Academy in 1945 and 1946, I had to walk from Napoleon Avenue to the Convent each day along St. Charles, and I usually took the middle of the neutral ground to try to escape falling caterpillars. From what I understand, caterpillars still plague people uptown in spring.

The only developed highway west from New Orleans to Baton Rouge was the *Airline,* with its hotels and bowling alleys and restaurants. Veterans Highway was not yet laid out. Lakeside Shopping Center was still part of the lake. Moisant Airport had only recently been dedicated.

The French Quarter was crowded with Italians, many of whom worked in the French Market. In the forties, Our Lady of Victory Church was called St. Mary's

Moisant International Airport served all major cities in this country and Central and South America.

The Times-Picayune Publishing Company faced Lafayette Square at the corner of Camp Street in the forties and fifties.

Italian Church because of the preponderance of Italians in the neighborhood. Montalbano's Grocery, where my Uncle Charlie liked to go for a wedge of Italian cheese cut from a huge wheel, was decorated with religious pictures, vigil lights, and a sign that changed each day to show the number of consecutive days of Masses Mr. Montalbano had attended.

In what is now *New Orleans East*, the string of camps that still stands in the lake today lined Hayne Boulevard, but there was little else. Everything was waiting on the I-10, still in the future, which would give access to the huge area.

The shops on *Canal Street*—Holmes, Maison Blanche, Godchaux's, Gus Mayer's, Kreeger's—were beautiful and their window displays were breathtaking. When ladies met for a shopping expedition, they always met "under the clock at Homezes," that's the way it was said. Canal Street theaters were like palaces. Trips to Canal Street still meant dressing up with hats and gloves. It was the best place in the city to shop, have lunch, or take in a movie. A good place to have lunch on a shopping day was at "Homezes" restaurant, sitting at the lunch counter. They made wonderful seafood gumbo. In the forties, as a teenager and a young married woman, I had little money, but I always found a quarter for a chunk of Heavenly Hash candy at the Maison Blanche candy counter to eat along the way.

In *Gentilly*, there were lots of split-shingle bungalows with porches that had been built in the thirties. No one had air-conditioning yet, so people still spent lots of time on their front porches. In Gentilly, the porches were screened, and you could sit there and rock and wield your palmetto fan without having to worry about the mosquitoes. Also in Gentilly, we began to see lawn decorations like pink flamingos standing on one foot and white wrought-iron cemetery benches.

Maison Blanche department store at the corner of Canal and Dauphine, 1949.

*A bus stops on Canal Street in front of Maison Blanche in the forties. (Courtesy
Louisiana Power & Light)*

Shops on Canal Street. By October 1943, Lerner's had moved one store over from K&B and Chandler's took its place.

Godchaux's at 141 Baronne.

A NEW ERA FOR THE CITY

Some things hadn't changed at all. The Sunday newspaper was still ten cents, if you bought it from the stands. A streetcar ride was still seven cents. And a Coke was still a nickel.

But some things were changing radically. On Sunday, May 5, 1946, New Orleans was staging a parade for its mayor-elect. The handsome young veteran from the silk-stocking crowd, deLesseps S. Morrison—called "Chep" by one and all—was to be inaugurated on Monday. The city was getting spruced up for the big day.

Mayor Morrison is about to present the Key to the City to Santa (Foxie Grisoli) on his traditional arrival in New Orleans at the head of the Christmas parade, 1948. (Courtesy May Glo Monteleone)

CHAPTER ELEVEN

Politics

Robert S. Maestri, mayor of New Orleans from 1936 to 1946, had a saying, "I got shaved without soap," meaning that someone had gotten the best of him. Undoubtedly, he made that remark on the morning of January 23, 1946, the day after he was defeated in the race for mayor by deLesseps S. ("Chep") Morrison.

"Them widow women beat me," Maestri said publicly. We can only wonder what he said privately.

The only man more surprised than Maestri that morning was the veteran candidate himself. Morrison, the "reform candidate," was young (thirty-three), handsome, and vigorous. He was just returning from a tour of duty in Europe as a colonel in the U.S. Army.

Before the war, Morrison had been practicing law. He had worked in the labor law section of the NRA, and had become a member of the state legislature in 1940, at the age of twenty-eight. Even though he was serving in Europe at the time, he'd been re-elected in 1944. Attractive to both women voters and veterans, he was a natural for politics. He agreed to enter the race for mayor, although he thought he had no chance whatsoever of winning.

A native of New Roads, Louisiana, Chep was the son of "Jake" Morrison (district attorney for Pointe Coupée, Iberville, and West Baton Rouge parishes) and the beautiful socialite Anita Olivier. Anita had been a Mardi Gras queen, and boasted a heritage including Ferdinand deLesseps, builder of the Suez Canal; Alderman Sidney Story, after whom the legalized "red-light" district Storyville had been named; and deLesseps Story, a respected New Orleans judge after whom Chep was named.

In 1939, Chep and his two law partners had created the "reform" League of Independent Voters. In 1939–40, they had endorsed Sam Houston Jones in his successful race for governor against Earl K. Long. Morrison had run for the state legislature on Jones' ticket and won.

In his race for mayor, Morrison had the endorsement of all the newspapers, who sent their best reporters to cover the "flaws" of the Maestri regime: the unpaid city bills, the obsolete fire equipment, the uncollected garbage, and the open gambling and prostitution. For forty-five days before the election, Morrison spoke to the people, projecting an image of reform. The fact that Maestri was unable to speak articulately in public was an embarrassment to him and a plus for the young veteran candidate.

THE STRENGTH OF "RING" POLITICS

Morrison knew that there were many voters in New Orleans who did not want gambling and prostitution stopped. He was also aware of the strength of "Ring" politics, which had been firmly entrenched in New Orleans since 1908 in the Martin Behrman years. Behrman used to say that with a nod, he could swing 25,000 votes. This was true. Such was the power of "Ring" politics.

The Old Regulars, Maestri's organization, *liked* the idea of opposing a reform candidate, who was usually inept and had no strong organizational support. Every four years, some such anti-"Ring" candidate would be offered up for the slaughter. It was traditional. No one expected such a candidate to win.

This time, however, the reformers were also supporters of former Governor Jones, who had broken the Long domination over Louisiana politics in 1940. They stressed the need for industrial expansion, and this reflected their civic concern and business awareness.

Women for Morrison, with brooms in hand, paraded down Canal Street, symbolizing the sweeping out of corruption. Veterans later joined the ladies in a door-to-door canvass of the city. The election was close, but it was a first primary victory.

ACHIEVEMENTS OF A YOUNG MAYOR

Housing for veterans was the number-one problem in the city. Mayor Morrison used his persuasive powers on the president of the Illinois Central Railroad, who had obtained the rights to Camp Plauché, the abandoned military base near New Orleans. The camp had streets, barracks, and recreational facilities, all ideal for civilian use. In June 1946, the conversion was begun and within two months, veterans began to occupy the 870-unit complex.

In September 1946, Morrison also proposed a city ordinance establishing the New Orleans Recreation Department. Basketball teams, football leagues, and instruction in other sports for the children of the city would be provided.

Then Morrison announced plans to use municipal bonds to finance two other proposed projects. One was a civic center complex, with a new city hall, library, auditorium, and other government buildings. The other was a Union terminal project, which would eliminate traffic tie-ups by routing nine railroad trunk lines presently using five railroad stations into one terminal. Plans for the terminal had begun under Maestri, but it was Morrison who was credited with the contract between city officials and the representatives of the railroad lines in 1947.

By the end of the decade, New Orleanians could point with pride to the achievements of their young mayor. New trade and industry had come to the city. Work on the Union terminal project and the civic center complex had begun, and NORD was a runaway success. So many street improvements, overpasses, and underpasses were being built that Morrison was dubbed "The Overpass King."

A rendering of the Union Passenger Terminal, drawn in the late forties. The terminal was dedicated in 1953.

The Elysian Fields overpass was completed under Morrison's administration.

Mayor Morrison (right) delivers proclamation to a dignitary in the late forties.

MORRISON ON "TOP TEN" LISTS

The successes of the dynamic young mayor received nationwide attention. In January of 1948, both the United States Junior Chamber of Commerce and the American Institute of Business Research put Morrison on their lists of the ten top young men in the country. *Time* magazine called him a "symbol of the bright new day which had come to the city of charming ruins, [who] symbolized as well as anyone or anything the postwar energy of the nation's cities." New Orleanians agreed.

THE SINGING GOVERNOR AND UNCLE EARL

Jimmie Davis, Louisiana's singing cowboy governor, was elected to two gubernatorial terms, 1944–48 and 1960–64. Davis, who wrote "You Are My Sunshine" and many other songs, was more famous for his singing than for any accomplishments while serving as governor.

He rarely gave speeches during his campaigns. Instead, he held rallies, where he and his band played his famous songs. Then he'd say a few words to the crowd, promising to be an honest governor. "I'd never do anything wrong," he said simply, "for life is too short and eternity too long to have to face your Maker with sins on your soul."

During his first term in office, his critics' principal complaint was that he spent too much time flying back and forth to Hollywood, where he had a night club, made records, and appeared in movies. One cowboy movie for which he was known was *Riding through Nevada,* made in 1943.

In 1948, Davis's term expired and he could not succeed himself. The next governor was Earl K. Long, younger brother of the late Senator Huey P. Long who had been assassinated in 1935. Earl K. Long liked to call Morrison "little old Dellasoups." This denigrating nickname was the least of the injuries he directed toward Morrison and the municipal government of New Orleans in the years 1948–52.

In 1948, Long defeated Sam Jones in the gubernatorial race. Davis had been a political associate of Jones, and consequently had political bonds with Morrison. He had tried, in his term of office, to cooperate with New Orleans by staying out of city affairs and permitting the mayor to act independently.

The 1948 gubernatorial primary revived the old conflict between good government and the Long style of government. Jones and Long opposed each other in this race just as they had in 1940, when it had been a campaign of moral indignation. Long was now fighting against not only Jones but also Morrison, the foremost Jones supporter. Morrison considered Jones the ideal man to keep harmony between the city and state governments. Morrison's endorsement strengthened the Jones organization, and for this, Long was determined to make Morrison pay.

In the rural parishes, Long spoke to his constituents dressed in baggy pants, red suspenders, and checkered shirts, chastising Morrison for his $400 suits and his cologne. He called Morrison "the little boy mayor." Like his brother the Kingfish, Earl took the role of the poor old country boy from Winn Parish who'd spent his early days in the cotton fields. He made fun of the city slickers. Many of the rednecks, poor blacks, and Cajuns in his audience responded to this kind of oratory.

Morrison, on the other hand, was the suave urbanite who had the family, education, and manners to put him in the top drawer of high society. This image was suited to his urban constituents.

Both men were ambitious and cunning politicians. For Morrison, the gubernatorial race was a fight for his own survival. On Long's inaugural day, Morrison, in an attempt to create an agreeable working relationship between city and state, sent flowers and his best wishes to Long, the incoming governor. But good wishes were not going to do it.

Although Long vowed not to hurt the city of New Orleans, he publicly derided the mayor, calling him "a boy in a man's job." Among his first priorities, Long listed the creation of a new political dictatorship and help for the Old Regulars in regaining power in New Orleans. To accomplish these goals, New Orleans had to be subjugated and Morrison had to be eliminated. He publicly asked Morrison to resign, but Morrison had no intention of doing so.

Louisiana constitutional law placed the government of New Orleans "under a special charter, subject to repeal or alteration at the whims of the legislature." This made New Orleans vulnerable to attack by the state. And in May 1948, the attack began. Two hundred bills were passed by the state legislature covering everything from firemen's pay in New Orleans to dog catching. Long's aims were to control the Port of New Orleans, modify New Orleans city government, precipitate a financial crisis in the city, and disrupt civil service. It was Huey Long all over again.

As long as Morrison and Long reigned concurrently, punitive legislation continued. But in June 1948, a 400-car motorcade led by Victor Schiro, who had organized the Young Men's Business Club, drove to the steps of the state capitol to protest and demand home rule for New Orleans. In 1950, New Orleans voters who resented Long's attacks and appreciated Morrison's achievements would go to the polls and re-elect "little old Dellasoups."

"GIVE-'EM-HELL" HARRY

Harry S. Truman became the thirty-third president of the United States on Thursday, April 12, 1945, just two and a half hours after Franklin Delano Roosevelt died of a cerebral hemorrhage at Warm Springs, Georgia. The former Jackson County farm boy was administered the oath of office, surrounded by the cabinet selected by his predecessor, high government officials, army and navy officers, and Democrats and Republicans in office. He told the press, "Boys, if you ever pray, pray for me now."

So overshadowed had he been as vice-president of the larger-than-life Roosevelt that when he became president, many Americans asked, "Harry Who?" And so stunned was Truman himself by his swift rise to world power that all he could do that first day was to ask the "Roosevelt Men" to stay on and promise them that he would carry on as he believed Roosevelt would have done.

President Truman loved this boner by the Chicago Daily Tribune *in 1948.*

Probably the greatest political upset in American history occurred when Truman defeated Thomas E. Dewey in the presidential election of 1948. The polls had predicted a landslide victory for Dewey. The Chicago *Tribune* had even prematurely reported in banner headlines that Dewey had won. But he hadn't. Truman had pulled off an extraordinary victory by bringing his campaign to the people through 31,000 miles of "whistle-stop" speeches.

In the newspapers, we saw pictures of Truman taking his morning "constitutionals," sometimes as early as 5:30 A.M. Secret Service agents surrounded him and newsmen followed, asking questions which he cheerfully answered.

"Look at him," my father said. Daddy was not one of his fans. "Smiling all the time. He doesn't have the sense to look worried."

At the time, as always in the past, I agreed with my father. Today, I think it was a good thing for him to smile, to appear confident. It gave the rest of the nation confidence. Looking back, having read and studied much about Truman, I consider him to have been a courageous and outstanding president.

Few presidents have ever been called upon to make such hard decisions or to take such unprecedented actions. And few have had such earth-shattering events happen during their administrations: dropping the bomb, the Truman Doctrine, the Berlin Airlift, the organization of the state of Israel and of NATO.

In the years after World War II, Truman was faced with pressures from big business and from the war-rich unions, who wanted freedom from government control in converting from wartime to peacetime economy. But Truman refused to budge. He didn't want to release controls too quickly, letting prices go sky high, which would have been bad for the ordinary citizen. By the same token, he wouldn't let the unions tie up the country with crippling strikes. He stood firm until the pendulum had time to swing. He courageously addressed the Senate, castigating big money interests who had "made their fortunes by spilling the blood of others." He managed to avoid massive unemployment and inflation and to keep America on an even keel during a difficult time.

A brick ranch-style home of the late 1940s.

CHAPTER TWELVE

Architecture and Interiors

IN THE LATE FORTIES, the suburban ranch house was establishing a foothold in new suburbs of New Orleans. This was a style that was strongly influenced by the prairie schoolhouses of Frank Lloyd Wright. They were built on concrete slabs with generous roof overhangs and carports.

In the late forties, in an area of Gentilly, the Higgins huts were coming down and slabs were being laid for a neighborhood that would be called Gentilly Woods, completed in 1950. They were pretty little weatherboard houses with two bedrooms and a bath, offered to GIs for almost no down payment and a thirty-year mortgage.

In Lakeview, houses were for the most part custom built on the undeveloped streets between Harrison Avenue and Robert E. Lee. The development of the new lakefront residential subdivisions had to wait on the demolition of military installations before streets and lots could be cut through and construction could begin. Only Lake Vista was ready for residential development, with lots cut to sell since 1938, and building material promised within a few months after the war. Lake Terrace would be finished in 1953, East and West Lakeshore by 1955 (replacing the Army and Navy hospitals), LSUNO Campus (now UNO) in 1958, and Lake Oaks in 1964.

SUBURBAN RANCH-STYLE HOUSES

Most of the houses built in Lakeview and Metairie in the late forties were also ranch-style houses, with facades three rooms wide. Many had carports. The lots were 50 feet by 100 or 120 feet. Suburban Ranch was the more accurate name, since they were built not in the inner city, like houses in the thirties, but in the suburbs.

Ranch-style houses were horizontal in appearance, with a low, wide facade that hugged the ground. The floor plans were L-shaped, U-shaped, or rectangular, with hipped or gabled roofs. A large picture window graced the central living room, flanked by ornamental shutters too small to cover the glass area, even if

Suburban ranch-style houses could be found in the late forties in Lakeview, Gentilly, Metairie, and Lakeshore subdivisions.

they had been hinged. The idea of the picture window was to bring the outdoors inside.

Carports and garages, single or double, put emphasis on the automobile and the suburbanite's ownership thereof. People wanted to own things. Cultural values were changing, and the carport exemplified the influence of these changes on architectural design.

LARGE FRONT LAWNS:
WHO DOES THE MOWING?

Also important to the ranch-style house was the large, well-manicured front lawn. Neighbors stood outdoors giving each other tips on using mulch and zoysia grass to grow thick, beautiful lawns. New Orleans was witnessing the birth of suburbia. Within a few years after the war, rows of lawns stretched out, green and velvety, for block after block in Lakeview and Metairie and Lake Vista. This of course meant maintenance, and many a homeowner paid for the prestige of having a beautiful lawn by pushing a manual lawn mower over this huge area once a week.

Television, as we shall see, invaded our lives in the late forties, making porches and verandas passé, exerting another influence on architectural design. Air-conditioning, even later, *kept* people indoors in hot weather, which in New Orleans was most of the year. Porches eventually disappeared from modern housing.

Milton H. Latter Memorial Library on St. Charles Avenue. The neo-Italianate mansion was built in 1907 by Marks Isaacs, founder of a major store on Canal Street. Silent-film star Marguerite Clark Williams once occupied it. Harry Latter, a real-estate baron, later bought it for $100,000. The Latters never lived there but donated it as a library on November 2, 1948, in honor of their son, Lt. Milton H. Latter (killed in action on Okinawa in World War II).

INTERIORS

The decor of older houses like my mother's could be classified as "sensible" in the forties. Hardwood floors with rugs (no wall-to-wall carpets), one settee, two "easy" chairs with ottomans, a console radio, a smoking stand: that was what made up the living room. The era for dens had not yet come. "Summer dress," with linen slipcovers on settees and chairs for a cooler feel than horsehair, was still very much in use. People also rolled up rugs and stored them in the summer, replacing them with rush mats or with nothing at all.

In the houses being built, the catchword was "functional." Everything was Danish modern, with square, armless chairs in the living room, and coffee tables and end tables with no scarves or embellishment. Hardwood floors were still being installed, and many were now in parquet design. Cornices gave the windows that clean, squared-off look.

Venetian blinds were all the rage, in new houses and old. Plastic was new and it was found in all sizes and shapes of dishes and kitchen utensils, toys and notions.

A beautiful living room in New Orleans in 1949, with venetian blinds and a hardwood floor. The woodburning fireplace, not popular in the decade, was blocked off.

"Functional" was the key word in decor in the forties. Here an ironing board pulls out of a bookshelf cabinet and a sewing machine swings out of a vanity.

Bay window of the forties. Venetian blinds were the rage. A space heater sits to the left, a smoking stand to the right.

A late forties playroom, with paneled walls, tiled floors, and blond furniture.

A kitchen of the period, with a modern stove and refrigerator, steel double sink, and chrome table legs.

This new house in 1949 had a dishwasher and disposal and venetian blinds. Metal cabinets were still in vogue.

In the kitchen, small appliances were limited, as was the counter space on which to put them. Toasters were universal. Some people had waffle irons. A few had electric mixers. Electric refrigerators were in general use, but no one I knew had a freezer. For laundry, many homes still had the wringer-type washing machine in the shed. Most homes had no clothes dryers, and neighbors still talked to each other as they hung their laundry. But new houses were being built with dishwashers and disposals, to the delight of the young housewife.

Ochsner Clinic opened its doors in 1942 on Prytania and Aline (3503 Prytania).

CHAPTER THIRTEEN

Progress in Science, Technology, and Medicine

NUCLEAR TECHNOLOGY

THE ATOM BOMB had ended the war. Our boys had come home from Europe and the South Pacific to pick up their lives, to be free from fear, to study, to work, to marry, to have children, to build houses. That is what the bomb had meant to us. But the atom bomb, we were learning, was more than just a couple of words on the front page of a newspaper, more than a nebulous and awe-inspiring concept.

The explosion of the atomic bomb was the climax of decades of study and experimentation that had begun in 1905 with a twenty-six-year-old high school dropout who had barely squeaked his way through college. His name was Albert Einstein. In 1905, he had written six extraordinary papers, changing the future of science, creating new fields of physics, and charting the course of atomic theory.

After the war, when I read about Einstein and the atom, I experienced a déjà-vu from my grammar-school days. Sr. Mary Henry was standing before the class, telling us that atoms were the source of energy.

"If the atom could be split," she'd said, "enough energy would be released to move the Empire State Building."

A hush had fallen over the class. Children loved extravagant stories, and this sounded like one. Then a dozen hands shot up.

"What *is* an atom?" one student asked.

"Why *can't* they split it?" someone else piped up.

"Where would they move the Empire State Building *to?*" a third wanted to know. I was that third student; I couldn't imagine why they'd want to move it in the first place.

The concept was light years beyond our grasp. Sister had few answers for us. Scientists didn't have a lot more. The field of nuclear physics was in its infancy (in the thirties), and the creation of an atomic bomb had not yet been contemplated.

After the war, many articles were published about Einstein and his theory of relativity, expressed in the formula $E = mc^2$. We were all glad to learn that only a handful of people in the world understood it. It made us feel less stupid. But with this simple (?) equation, this man of peace made many important discoveries possible, as well as the thermonuclear bomb.

MEDICAL ADVANCEMENTS

My sister Terry was born in 1944. She was the only one of my mother's children to be taken for regular visits to a pediatrician. Perhaps other mothers had done this earlier, but *my* mother hadn't had a baby in ten years, and all this was new to her. Mother took Terry for her shots, including DPT (diphtheria, pertussis, tetanus) when they were due. She had a hard time getting past my "no-change" father for those injections.

"I can't see injecting a perfectly healthy child with bacteria, so she can become immune to a disease," he argued. This was before Mother had embarked upon this new and daring medical procedure. "It's a wonder they don't all get sick right after the shots. Maybe they do. You don't know." Mother didn't know, but she trusted her doctor, and she went ahead with the injections.

Neither Elaine nor Bill nor Terry, my three younger siblings, ever had to sweat out a fever under a mustard plaster, as Bob and I had. The miracle drugs came along just in time for them to escape that medieval torture.

The dye sulfanilamide had been synthesized as early as 1908, but it was not until 1932 that a derivative, prontosil, was tested against streptococcal infection in mice and rabbits. Its success was miraculous. In 1933, it was used in human beings for the treatment of blood poisoning. The way was now open for antibiotics in what would be a medical revolution.

Alexander Fleming had discovered penicillin in 1928, but all through the thirties it remained a curiosity, with no practical application. It still remained for pure penicillin to be isolated by Howard Florey and Ernst Chain in 1939 before techniques could be devised for mass production. It was first used by the military during the war; later it became available to civilians.

In 1944, tuberculosis was effectively treated by streptomycin. From that time on, medicine became a whole new profession, bent on curing disease through biomedical science.

The big focus was on research, accelerated principally by the war and the need for medication for the treatment of wounded servicemen. By 1950 and the Korean War, the use of penicillin and the mycins was widespread, as was the availability of the drugs.

Another important medical advancement in 1948 was the treatment of arthritis by the use of cortisone.

In the late forties, French neurosurgeon Henri Laborit asked the laboratories to come up with an antihistamine to calm his patients prior to anaesthesia. They came up with a drug called chlorpromazine, which produced such a "euphoric quietude" that he recommended it to his colleagues who treated manic depressives. With these patients, it again achieved miraculous effects. It was later discovered effective in the treatment of schizophrenia.

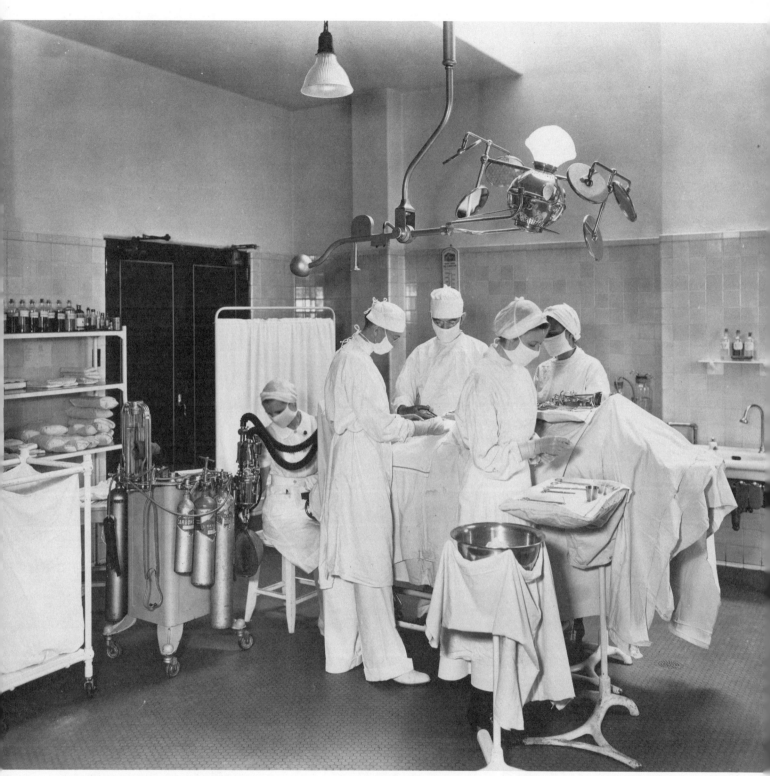

A typical operating room in 1944.

OCHSNER CLINIC

In New Orleans, a clinic was founded in 1941 that was to gain worldwide recognition as a treatment and diagnostic center. Started by five surgeons, it was named after one of them, Dr. Alton Ochsner. The others were Dr. Edgar Burns, urologist; Dr. Curtis Tyrone, obstetrician/gynecologist; Dr. Francis LeJeune, ENT specialist; and Dr. Guy Caldwell, orthopedic surgeon. Dr. Ochsner became a world-renowned surgeon and teacher as well as the first modern physician to draw a connection between cigarette smoking and cancer of the lung.

The Ochsner Clinic, organized as a private partnership, opened its doors on Aline and Prytania on January 2, 1942. Nineteen physicians were listed as staff members or consultants on the original staff roster. For hospital facilities, the doctors first used beds in the Touro Infirmary, across the street from the clinic. Then, in 1946, they established their own hospital in the old army barracks under the Huey P. Long Bridge. This they referred to affectionately as "Splinter Village."

The Ochsner Foundation Hospital has been located at its present site on Jefferson Highway adjacent to Ochsner Clinic since 1954.

THE DIGITAL COMPUTER

Wars traditionally spawn technological advances, and because the need for a particular machine or device is more crucial then, research is speeded up. One of the marvels of modern technology that came out of World War II was the digital computer. In Great Britain, mathematician Alan Turing helped design an electronic computer in secrecy, one which would crack the Nazi code machine, "Enigma." Put into use in 1943, it was considered a principal factor in Germany's defeat, for the Nazis never knew that this computer—called Colossus—was cracking their codes as fast as they were turning them out.

Back in 1943, physicist John William Mauchly and a twenty-two-year-old engineer, J. Presper Eckert at the University of Pennsylvania, started building the first general-purpose computer called Eniac (Electronic Numerical Integrator and Computer). I was in college at the time, doing my term papers on a portable typewriter, making typos and having to type whole pages over again. Little did I dream that this miracle machine was on its way. As I sit here four decades later at my Hyundai computer, I sometimes marvel at its ability to take complicated orders at the touch of a button and carry them out so swiftly and efficiently. I sometimes forget that 90 percent of the order I'm giving to "save the material" I've typed or to "print it" or "move it" is already preprogrammed into this remarkable machine. It needs only one final touch of a button to set it on its way to the accomplishment of that task.

In 1945, the computer was put to work calculating bomb and missile trajectories for the army, doing a job that had previously taken the labor of 200 people using desk-top calculating machines.

Since then, computers have improved so dramatically in vacuum tubes, transistors, integrated circuits, micro processor chips, and memory devices, that there is no resemblance whatsoever between the giant monoliths of the forties and the attractive TV-like terminals used in homes today. This miracle of modern technology that has made it possible to store institutional billing and records, as well as life-saving medical statistics (information formerly kept in space-consuming and hard-to-find folders), was a product of the war in the forties.

OTHER DISCOVERIES

By the war's end, the vacuum tubes of Lee de Forest's radio had also been crucial to the development of radar—an advancement that saved thousands of lives. What a wonderful device to be developed from something that looked like a fancy light bulb!

Leo Baekeland, an eccentric millionaire, invented something in his last years that was to change life in the twentieth century: plastics. He was the father of polyester, polyvinyl, polystyrene, many other "polys," and greatest of all, nylon. His Bakelite would not melt, could resist acids, and was a superb electrical insulator. It found use in toasters, pot handles, and electric plugs, as well as airplane parts, automobile parts, and radio parts. His plastics created major industries and revolutions in already existing industries. Manufacturers knew that his creations would toughen, lighten, and diversify their products.

In the thirties and forties, the plastics industry established itself as indispensable. As Baekeland was withdrawing from the world in senility, other scientists were taking his polymer into new areas. One morning in May 1940, less than four years before his death, more than four million pairs of nylon stockings went on sale, and in four days almost all were bought up. I personally do not remember seeing a pair of nylon stockings until 1945.

The WDSU-TV antenna atop the Hibernia Bank Building (1948), later moved to Chalmette. Television impulses were beamed from the location of the camera to the antenna, and then to television sets all over the city. (Courtesy Paul Yacich)

CHAPTER FOURTEEN

Television, the Eighth Wonder of the World

THE FIRST TELEVISION program broadcast in New Orleans was a remote from the Municipal Auditorium on December 18, 1948 over WDSU-TV, with a host of Hollywood stars. After that, word began to spread about the marvels of television, and about the programs that were being broadcast over our new New Orleans station. Since WDSU-TV Channel 6 was the first and only station in town, it received programs on film from all four networks: NBC, ABC, CBS, and Dumont, and relayed them to local audiences at regularly scheduled times. Like most New Orleanians, we didn't have a television set yet, but it would not be long in coming.

My father had been a radio hobbyist back in the twenties, when the radio was still a "toy." He had put together one of the early "crystal sets" and considered radio a wonder without equal, for it had given us access to news, sports, entertainment, and a look at the national scene, which had broadened all our horizons. He remained a loyal listener long after television had taken over the homes and become the nation's chief source of entertainment.

My mother and father had taken a trip to New York in 1939 and seen the first commercial television displayed at the World's Fair. But it was not until after the war that materials became available for mass production.

My Memere, my mother's mother, who lived with us, was the first one in *our* home to say she wanted a television set. Her neighbors and nieces told her every day about the wonderful shows they were seeing with comedians and dancers and singers, and she was determined to enjoy that entertainment.

Daddy would have been content with his radio forever, or so he thought at the time. And Mother did pretty much whatever Daddy said. But Memere was another county to be heard from. She had her own money, and she was going to buy a television set, and those who wanted to watch it could do so. So she put on her hat, took the streetcar to Canal Street, bought a set, and had it delivered to the house. It was a huge console model with a ten-inch screen and a round

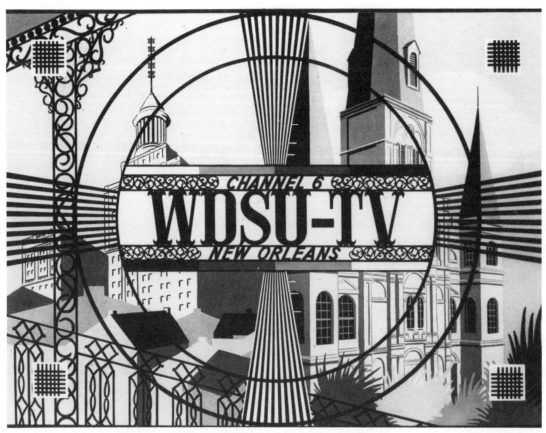

This WDSU-TV test pattern showed on your screen if no program was on. (Courtesy Paul Yacich)

bubble glass, and although it showed programs for only a few hours each evening, we thought it was the eighth wonder of the world.

This was in 1949, when I was still working as a service rep at the Telephone Company and Al was still at Loyola. We were still living on Orleans Street with Mother and Daddy and Memere and my younger siblings Elaine (seventeen), Bill (fifteen), and Terry (four). At night, we all crowded into the living room (joined by my aunt and uncle who lived upstairs) to watch the evening programs.

With a chip on his shoulder, Daddy settled himself in his bedroom with his radio, lit his pipe, and cracked open his evening newspaper. The rest of the family could sit around that box all night if they liked, but he had no intention of giving up his "Amos 'n Andy," and his "Fibber McGee and Molly" just because some old vaudevillians were doing pratfalls in a make-shift studio. What was the matter with people, anyway? Were they all going crazy or something?

It was months before he grudgingly joined us for some particular program, explaining in advance that it was an educational show about nature or science or . . . something.

There were no daytime programs in the beginning. Programming started at 2:00 or 3:00 in the afternoon and ran until maybe 10:30 at night. But the appeal of the box was so strong, we'd get up in the morning and turn on the TV and watch the test pattern. I guess many others did the same because one day I remember seeing the test pattern with this message: "This test pattern is brought to you by D. H. Holmes." Holmes had actually bought time on the test pattern.

UNCLE MILTIE, THE FIRST TV SUPERSTAR

At work on Tuesdays, all we could talk about was the Texaco Star Theater with Milton Berle, which came on on Tuesday nights. Everyone raced home and rushed through dinner and the dishes to get settled in a comfortable chair for the program. When the four uniformed gas-station attendants began their opening song, we nearly burst with excitement.

We started giggling during the commercial, in anticipation of a terrific hour of entertainment right in our own home, and best of all, free! Then out from behind the curtains came "Uncle Miltie," dressed up in one of his outrageous costumes. He would walk on the insides of his arches and make a buck-toothed face for the camera, while everyone howled. He was television's first superstar, and his universal popularity sold millions of television sets in the years to come. In his weekly variety program, he sang, danced, did imitations, and told jokes, for the monumental salary of $6,500 a week.

"Who could possibly be worth that kind of money?" my father asked. But Daddy couldn't hold out forever. Even *he* fell under the spell of Uncle Miltie. And later, he had no choice but to give in, when his old radio favorites moved over to television: Fibber McGee and Molly, George Burns and Gracie Allen, Jack Benny and Mary Livingston, and Molly Goldberg.

TV HAD ITS OWN STARS

But TV introduced its own stars. Ed Sullivan started in the late forties with his "Toast of the Town" variety show. A former newspaper columnist, Sullivan introduced many beginners like Wayne Newton and, later on, Elvis Presley and the Beatles. A spot on his show was tantamount to success in television. Then came "The Ted Mack Amateur Hour," Kate Smith, Ed Wynn, the ventriloquist Paul Winchell and his dummy Jerry Mahoney, and even John Forsythe. As the radio comedian Fred Allen said, "They all looked like a collection of passport photos." But to us it was still a miracle.

In the forties, William Boyd, an old movie cowboy, cut up some of his "Hopalong Cassidy" movies and showed them on TV as a series.

A new suppertime show for kids was "Howdy Doody," with Buffalo Bob, where Bob opened the show by asking, "Say, kids! What time is it?" A sound track answered, "It's Howdy Doody time."

For musical entertainment, we had Fred Waring and his Pennsylvanians. For drama, there was the Philco Theater and the Kraft Theater, both over NBC.

Since this was simple entertainment brought into the home, it included no excessive violence and no sex whatsoever, except for an occasional modest kiss.

WDSU-TV, THE FIRST LOCAL TV STATION

In December 1948, when WDSU-TV began beaming out television programs to those lucky few who had television sets in New Orleans, the station was not yet in the spacious studios at 520 Royal Street. After obtaining a construction permit and installing their antenna atop the Hibernia Bank Building, they started broadcasting from a studio that was one room on the fourteenth floor of the Hibernia. In years to come, the antenna would be moved to Chalmette, where it remains today.

Paul Yacich, left, engineer for WDSU-TV, puts the first antenna together to be set atop the Hibernia Bank Building in 1948. Carlos Dodd faces the camera, with an unidentified helper. They assembled the antenna in an empty freight yard on Annunciation Street, where a Schwegmann supermarket stands today. (Courtesy Paul Yacich)

The original staff of WDSU-TV, the first television station in New Orleans. This was taken in the Brulatour Courtyard in 1950, but everyone in it was there from the beginning, December 1948. Seated: Charles Flotte, engineer; Birda Price, maintenance; Connie Green, traffic; Lydia Otto, accounting; Irwin Poche, director; Edwin Tong, assistant chief engineer. Standing: Ken Muller, director; Aaron Andrus, engineer; Edgar Stern, owner; Lindsey Riddle, chief engineer; A. B. Suhor, head of accounting; J. Lowell Otto, engineer; Paul Yacich, engineer; John Muller, first director. (Courtesy Paul Yacich)

The industry was so new that most of the men who were going to run the station had never even seen a television set, much less a station. Paul Yacich, an engineer with the station from the start, later a director, said, "I went to New York in 1948 and sat in Jack Dempsey's, one of the few places that showed television day and night, and watched the set for two weeks, just to see what it was like and to study the programs.

"For almost a year, we practiced programs at Werlein's, doing interview shows and programs like 'Mid-Day,' getting ready to go on the air, but none of this was broadcast."

My husband and his friend Forrey Villarrubia used to work part-time for Maison Blanche in the "New Business" department, while they were going to college on the G.I. Bill. One of their duties was to carry merchandise from Maison Blanche to the Hibernia Bank Building to a young lady named Gay Leonardo, who wrote and acted in commercials for Maison Blanche over WDSU-TV. Gay spread the merchandise out on a table in the "studio," and described each item as the cameraman zoomed in on it. These commercials were shown at the breaks in the wrestling matches.

Gay represented Maison Blanche and Terry Flettrich represented D. H. Holmes. They even called Terry "Helen Holmes." Terry was fashion coordinator for Holmes in the late forties, and her face was often seen on Channel 6. She also did TV specials for Holmes like "The Holmes State Review," which she made with her photographer husband, Leonard Flettrich, in 1949. Early in the fifties, she came to work for the TV station when she took over the "Mid-Day Show."

I learned a lot of stories recently about the first television studio in the Hibernia Bank Building. For one show, they wanted the piano to revolve, so they put it on a turntable and two men got down on the floor and turned it manually while the camera rolled.

"The room was so small," Mel Leavitt told me, "that if you needed a medium shot, the cameraman had to roll the camera back into the corridor. For a long shot, he had to back into the ladies' room across the hall."

Terry Flettrich, one of New Orleans' earliest TV personalities, with artist-photographer husband, Leonard T. Flettrich. They are pictured here on top of the Hibernia Bank Building, working on "The Holmes State Parade" for WDSU-TV in 1948. (Courtesy Terry Flettrich Rohe)

Naomi ("Nonie") Bryant on her show "Spot the Stars," broadcast from the Channel 6 studio in the Hibernia Bank Building in 1949. Woody Leafer, one of the station's first announcers, did skits with her on the show. (Courtesy Paul Yacich)

In the new WDSU-TV studio on Royal Street, Mel Leavitt gets ready for a program. Left to right: two visitors, cameraman George Cuccia, director Irwin Poche, Mel Leavitt, unidentified person, cameraman Mel Price, and Buddy Rizzuto. (Courtesy Paul Yacich)

EARLY LOCAL STARS

One of the first local television stars I remember was Naomi ("Nonie") Bryant, who had her own show called "Spot the Stars." She was a singer and actress, perhaps the first woman on television in New Orleans. She used to sing songs from by-gone decades, and viewers would call in to say which singer had made the song famous. She also did skits with an announcer called Woody Leafer. I recall that she later had another program, a quiz show called "Grade-A Kids," with bright grammar-school children who answered questions. This was sponsored by a dairy company.

Another early local TV personality was Mel Leavitt, who has been a sports and special events commentator in New Orleans for over forty years. Mel covered sports events and did remote broadcasts from the Fair Grounds Racetrack, the Audubon Zoo, the Coliseum Arena, baseball parks, and football stadiums. He was also one of the first to cover the Mardi Gras parades, giving a description of each float and explaining its significance in the theme of the parade. This was a boon to the elderly who could not get out to watch these well-loved spectacles. Mel's face became well known in New Orleans, and after he married Naomi Bryant, they became a "show-biz" couple to the people of the city, as glamorous as any Hollywood stars.

I remember reading that Nonie had gotten her first big break when she sang one night at Lenfant's. It was a place where young talent was showcased. Pete Fountain and George Gerard played there in the Basin Street Six. After her appearance at Lenfant's, she was offered her own show on WDSU-TV.

Another early star on the local scene was Vera Massey, a lady who was the hostess of a program called "Our House," the forerunner of the "Mid-Day Show."

Announcers in 1949 were Fred Paul, Dick Bruce, Byron Dowtey, Rex Moad, Woody Leafer, Joe Fribley, and Roger Wolfe. Carl Junker was director of operations in 1949. WDSU-TV would be the only television station in New Orleans for the next nine years.

As the forties ended and the fifties began, WDSU-TV moved to its new location at 520 Royal Street and entered the fabulous age of television that was just about to begin. Channel 6 was a part of it right from the start.

The turban and "good little suit" of the war years.

CHAPTER FIFTEEN

Fashions and Fads

FASHIONS IN WOMEN'S CLOTHES

BEFORE THE WAR, American dress designers had always looked to Paris to lead the way in styles and fabrics of dresses. But after France was occupied in 1940, our designers were on their own, and the decisions were theirs alone.

In addition, the government laid down some regulations, restricting the amount of fabric that could be used by dress manufacturers. A dress could have no more than two inches in the hem. It could have only one patch pocket, no attached hoods or shawls, and no belt over two inches wide. No skirt could measure more than seventy-two inches around. So, although we consumers didn't know it at the time, there was good reason why *Vogue*, *Harper's Bazaar*, and *Glamour* promoted the "good little suit" as an answer to wartime shortages.

The suit, with its slim skirt, short jacket, and soft blouse, could be worn to work, dinner, or dancing. "Whatever you may be doing, short of hoeing your Victory Garden," said *Vogue* in its February 15, 1944 edition, "you may be . . . quite correctly . . . wearing a suit."

In the war years, dress designers borrowed ideas from war-uniform manufacturers. The Eisenhower jacket was softened when made of crepe with a drawstring waist. Copies of the Women's Army Corps cap and the British tank corps beret were dressed up with sequins to top off a suit. Evening gowns, draped over one hip, were designed with an eagle's wing in gold spread diagonally from shoulder to waist.

For four years, American women wore suits made with an economy of fabric. But when the war ended, and Paris was freed, a dress designer named Christian Dior turned American fashion, indeed world fashion, upside down. Everything women had worn in the war years was now out-of-date; the only "in" style was the exciting "New Look."

Dior's dresses were divine. The swirling skirts were not only fuller but longer, with hems only twelve inches from the floor. The Joan Crawford shoulder pads

149

Dressed up to go downtown shopping. Note the shirtwaist dress with shoulder pads and the hem just below the knee, before the New Look of the late forties.

which had been worn in everything in the early forties now disappeared. Dior's "New Look" emphasized the soft shoulder, the slender waist, the full bosom and hips, and his voluminous skirts gave a hint of slender legs. The skimpy wartime look was gone.

By 1949, under a fashionable suit which had a tight jacket and an immensely full skirt, a lady wore a garter belt—no more roll garters—a pair of nylon hose, and an all-in-one bra and corset, made of bones that encased her from her breast to her hips. Over that was a silk slip and a number of crinolines holding out her skirt to its proper width. This was elegance.

Women went mad for the "New Look." They wanted to throw out everything they had and buy a whole new wardrobe, but who could afford it? Husbands were up in arms. In Dallas, even women banded together, over one thousand strong, protesting in the "Little-Below-the-Knee Club." A style revolution was underway.

Wholesale dress manufacturers in New York, and eventually in New Orleans, did what they'd always done. They copied Dior's "New Look" creations, turning out thousands of copies at $20 apiece. The classic suit dress with sloping shoulders and curving waistline sold for $19.95. An afternoon dress of blue-and-white tie silk was $14.95. An off-the-shoulder taffeta cocktail dress was $17.95.

When nylon became available, we all considered it a miracle. Imagine a whole dress made of a fabric that could be folded in a suitcase overnight and taken out without a wrinkle! Imagine a dress you could rinse out at night to dry, wrinkle-free, before morning! "The end of ironing!" we wanted to shout from the housetops. We could buy nylon dresses in prints, stripes, and flowered designs. And so what if the fabric did not breathe and made you perspire in the summer? Nothing was perfect.

Bathing suits of the period.

Playclothes were big in the war years, since they satisfied our yearnings for something new on the fashion scene and required little fabric. A grown-up romper suit, for example, was an all-in-one playsuit including a blouse and a wrap-around diaperlike garment, with ruffles. It was cute and feminine and it met all government regulations.

In 1942, when I started Loyola, I made myself three peasant skirts, also called umbrella skirts, with three yards of fabric each (at thirty-nine cents a yard from Kress). I would wear these to school with my white sport blouses, holdovers from my high-school convent uniforms. A year later, if I'd bought these skirts ready-made, there would have been only two yards in each (government regs).

Zippers—then called slide fasteners—were impossible to get after 1943, for they were then all made of metal. Meeting the challenge, designers came up with wraparound skirts. Before the war, ads had tried to entice women to buy zippers, saying that a woman had "gap-osis" without them—her skirt "gapped" between hooks or buttons on her hip. Zippers were far from universal in the late thirties. Then, just when we had begun to think we couldn't get along without them, we had to learn to do just that.

Shorts and halters were popular during the war, as were peasant blouses and three-piece playsuits, consisting of a blouse, a pair of shorts, and a button-down-the-front skirt, all of the same material.

High school and college girls wore "Sloppy-Joe" sweaters. They were long-sleeved pullovers, made in a solid color, and worn large with a pleated plaid skirt. Our only adornment was a string of pearls.

A college co-ed in a sweater, skirt, and pearls.

For lounging at home, we wore jeans with men's dress shirts, the tails tied together in front. Sometimes a regular sport shirt was worn, with a flannel shirt over it.

ACCESSORIES

I can never remember getting a new outfit in the forties without getting a hat, purse, shoes, and gloves to match. Since this was an expensive proposition, and since shoes were rationed anyway, we all began buying dresses or suits to "go with" accessories we already had. But after the war, the lid was off, and shoe styles, among other things, went crazy.

Since we were wearing longer hemlines, our shoes had to be extravagant to call attention to our legs. Popular in the late forties were shoes with open toes, ankle straps, spike heels, and clunky platforms. For teenagers, saddle oxfords and loafers with bobby sox were "the thing," as were huaraches without socks or stockings.

No woman in the forties considered herself really dressed without a hat, whether she was going shopping, to church, to dinner, or to a movie. Women's hats in the forties were feminine and highly extravagant, with wide brims, giant flowers, and draped and pleated fabrics. Some were in the shape of pillboxes worn on the front of the head, bird's nests, blown-up derbies, and starbursts of peacock feathers. Of course, there were still the conventional mushroom hats, pinwheels, and pancake straws.

Turbans were very popular. The story was told that Ann Sheridan, the movie star, had a date one night to go dancing at a Hollywood night spot and her hair was a mess. So she cut a wide strip of fabric and wrapped it around her head, and the turban was born. Every woman had to have one . . . or many.

Let's go shopping!

Styles of the forties—dresses with short jackets, high-heeled white shoes, bows in hair.

Bandanas, snoods, and fascinators (crocheted triangular scarves) were sometimes worn in place of hats.

Gauntlet gloves were popular, and so were narrow, elbow-length gloves. It was
an era when *more* was *better.*

It was also a decade when everything had to match. Matching hats and bags
were manufactured in stripes, pleats, and other variations. Spider-web blouses
were cute with their matching spider-web parasols, if you didn't go blind looking
at them.

UNDERGARMENTS

Women wanted a bare-shouldered look. This called for a new strapless wired
bra, which came out in 1946, when wire was once again available.

During the war, ladies' panties had been made of rayon, with a split at the side
and a button at the waistline. No elastic was available. But with the end of the
war, we soon had nylon panties with elastic waistbands, a luxury we had never
known before.

I only had one pair of nylon stockings on December 29, 1945, the day I got
married. Almost as soon as the war was over, signs began to appear—"Limited
Sale of Nylon Hosiery, Saturday Only"—and the line would form before the
store opened. I think the manufacturers had them all through the war but
wouldn't have put them on sale, for fear of looking unpatriotic, since nylon was
used for parachutes and for towlines for gliders. So I waited in line to get my "one
to a customer" just in time for my wedding day.

During the war, we'd worn rayon hose or Queen's Lace hose which were stylish
and pretty, but they did not cling, especially since they were held up by roll
garters. Instead, they settled in little pools of spidery webs around our ankles. So
it is easy to understand how happy we were with our nylon hose, and our nylon
panties and bras and slips—all no-iron!

HAIRDOS

After a brief romance with the short Victory bob in the early forties, I went
back to the shoulder-length hairstyle, and so did most of my friends. The Victory
bob needed no bobby pins, they said, and bobby pins, along with everything else,
had gone to war. But the truth of the matter was that short hair needed to be "put
up" in bobbies even more than long hair did. Short *straight* hair, we discovered,
was terrible, and we were still decades away from the blow dryer.

My picture, taken in 1942 and used as the frontispiece of the Loyola 1943
yearbook, shows me with a Victory bob. But in my wedding picture in 1945, my
hair was once again long, and worn in swirls. For this hairdo, only the hair at the
back half of the head had to be put up in curls. The swirls at the front were
secured to the head with bobby pins.

Usually a side part allowed for a big swirl on one side and a smaller swirl on the
other—both augmented by teasing or "rats," which gave height to the hairline.
Many of my friends wore flat-topped hairdos, center or side-parted, and brushed
back into soft waves held in place by bobby pins, then falling loosely to the
shoulder.

For a date, a young woman often ornamented her hair with a fresh flower, a
feather, or a flat black velvet bow (a la Rose Marie of the old "Dick Van Dyke

Vivien, soloist on "The Hour of Charm" (sponsored by New Orleans Public Service), sports the fashion and hairstyle of the forties. (Courtesy Louisiana Power & Light)

A Victory bob, red lips and nails, and shoulder pads were marks of the war years.

A working girl of the forties.

Second generation Batt boys (sons of the Batt brothers, who managed Pontchartrain Beach Amusement Park) with dates and friends cut dashing figures. Left to right: Harry Batt, Jr., Fay Villac, Richard Batt, Jr., Joan Boudousquié, Junior Miss New Orleans Eloys Langhoff, John Batt, Alberta, John Kleinpeter (July 1946). (Courtesy Joan Garvey)

Show") instead of a hat. Also for formal evenings, the upsweep hairdo added glamor. The hair was brushed up from the neckline, secured at the crown of the head with bobby pins and rolled into dozens of curls, which created a "bouquet" effect. Betty Grable was known for this hairdo, and her pile of curls was so high and so thick, it seemed it would take quite a job of balancing to keep the head erect.

COSMETICS

Powder, rouge, and lipstick were all most women used in the forties. Eye makeup was not in general use, except by young women who had blonde hair and fair eyelashes. They used Maybelline mascara, which came in a little red box with a tiny brush. The brush was dampened and rubbed across the mascara and then applied to the brows and lashes.

We all plucked our eyebrows, however—not to the pencil-thin Claudette Colbert brow, but we didn't leave them as thick as Brooke Shields, either. We tried to define an arch in a brow of moderate thickness, leaving no wandering hairs unplucked. Our eye makeup consisted of a moistened finger applied to the brows and lashes to remove the excess face powder.

Foundation makeup was, at that time, pancake makeup that came in a little can resembling a shoe polish can and containing a thin flat sponge. The sponge was dampened and passed across the cake of makeup, then smoothed across the face. Few young women I knew wore pancake makeup.

Lipstick was bright red or dark red. Rouge was cake rouge applied with a puff. Powder was bought in a shade to match your skin color, prepared by Coty or Max Factor. Fingernail polish usually matched your lipstick. In the war years, fingernails were still being painted with the moons left white and the nail painted white at the tips, like the "new" French manicure of the eighties. But it took a skillful manicurist to do a good job with this difficult work of art.

At the telephone company, I began to be aware of fragrances I enjoyed on other young women. I sought out colognes like Tweed and Toujours Moi and Evening in Paris.

COSTUME JEWELRY

Before the war, Audrey and I and our friends wore a single piece of good jewelry around our necks—a gold cross and chain or a string of pearls. We wore a watch and a ring, either a birthstone or a monogram ring, and little other jewelry. But after the war, costume jewelry became a big industry. Women had an insatiable appetite for new styles, crazy fashions, and clunky costume jewelry. Eisenberg pins and earrings were designed of huge, cut-lustre stones in a new American technique, and they were the rage.

Clip-on earrings were popular throughout the forties, but pierced ears were once again also in vogue. My mother had had her ears pierced when she was a teenager, but the style had vanished, and so had the holes in her earlobes. I had my ears pierced just before I graduated from Loyola in 1945. Before I took the plunge, however, I walked down Royal Street and looked in the windows of the antique shops in search of a pair of antique earbobs, and I found them. They were old gold drop earrings for pierced ears, each set with a fine pearl. I asked my mother and father to give them to me for my graduation. Then I paid a visit to the doctor, held my breath, and had my ears pierced. I wore the earrings almost daily, even on my wedding day, and I wear them still.

Dressed up for work in the mid-1940s.

Those who designed men's clothes looked to New York and Hollywood for their inspiration. The market for their creations was limited to the male population not wearing uniforms for Uncle Sam for four years.

California dictated styles in men's sport clothes like slack suits with matching shirts, men's shorts for tennis, and the elimination of swimsuit tops. Hawaiian shirts were popular, reflecting the desire for more color in men's clothing.

Suits were frequently made with two pairs of trousers, one matching the coat, one contrasting. Suit coats were single or double-breasted. In the early forties, coats had shoulder pads; after the war, they followed the natural line of the shoulder. Because of a shortage of fabric during the war, coats were made without patch pockets or vests. Tuxedo coats followed the lines of suit coats but were black. A white dinner jacket was worn with black trousers, a black bow tie, and a cummerbund. After the war, wine and blue tuxedos were seen. Tails were sometimes worn for evening, some in navy blue.

Trousers were pleated at the waist and full about the leg. Slacks were now worn for golf instead of knickers. After the war, all trousers had zippers for fastenings, instead of buttons or clasps. Cuffs appeared. Denim was used in blue, grey, and brown for wash slacks. Blue jeans were popular, and Bermuda shorts were introduced.

Shirts were coat style with stays in collars to prevent curling. French cuffs were popular on dress shirts. Shirts were made of broadcloth, chambray, and oxford cloth. Dark colors gained popularity: maroon, navy, brown, and wine, worn with light colored coats and trousers. Polo shirts, crew necks, and boat neck shirts appeared on the style scene.

After the war, all colors were popular. Open-neck shirts were worn with a scarf or a muffler. Knit shirts and T-shirts were popular for casual wear. Sport shirts were worn in or out of the trousers for casual wear.

Ties were still four-in-hand for daytime wear. Also seen were hand-painted ties in Hawaiian prints. The Windsor knot came into vogue, as well as the wool knit tie. After the war, the ready-tied bow tie appeared.

Oxfords were worn for work; canvas shoes for the beach. After the thirties, high-top shoes were not seen except on old men. Penny loafers were popular for lounging, and sandals for casual wear. After the war, there were crepe soles, flight boots, moccasins, and for dress, the wing-tip shoe.

Overcoats were calf-length with a narrow V and a military line. After the war, the natural shoulder line developed.

Hats had been universally popular during the Depression and until the war. They were soft felts with a snap brim for winter, Derby hats, and Panama straws for summer. Caps were worn for golfing and boating.

Men's hair still had the "wet head" look of water and brilliantine. It was worn short with a side part and cut high over the ears and at the neckline, with only a trace of sideburns. Very few men wore beards or moustaches in the forties.

Jewelry consisted of pocket watches, wristwatches, a collar pin under the tie to hold the collar points, a tie bar, a wedding ring, a class or signet ring, an ID bracelet, cuff links, a fraternity pin, and a monogram belt buckle.

Underwear and pajamas were made of sanforized cotton. Pajamas were coat style or belted Cossack style. Men wore woolen or cotton bathrobes, calf-length and belted. The first boxer shorts and T-shirts had come out in the thirties, but

For dress-up, a double-breasted pinstripe with a pocket handkerchief was spiffy in 1946.

When young couples gathered to play bridge, men wore coats and ties and women wore stockings and high heels.

boxer shorts with elastic all around were introduced after the war. Swimsuits appeared in latex with Hawaiian designs.

Belts, billfolds, pocket handkerchiefs, garters, gloves, umbrellas, plastic-rimmed or rimless glasses, and suspenders were common. After 1945, all men's garments were fuller cut and ensembles enjoyed much popularity. Overalls and coveralls were abandoned as work clothes in favor of slacks and T-shirts or sport shirts. Many men stopped wearing undershirts by the end of the decade. Colors and ornamental extras were much sought after in men's wear.

FADS OF THE FORTIES

The zoot suit: This was the butt of many jokes by radio comedians. Comic strips also poked fun at it. But in truth, it was rarely seen. It was a novelty, a costume, not a regular mode of dress. The coat was made with exaggerated shoulder pads,

Dresses of the forties, with a young man wearing a "zoot suit."

lapels, and length. The pants were high-waisted, held up with suspenders, and pleated with what the young people called a "reet pleat." The pants legs were full, narrowing at the ankle, and draped from waist to pocket with a watch chain sometimes five feet long. The dress shirt was decorated with a wide bow tie.

In this outfit, supposedly, the "hep-cat" jitterbugged the night away. This outfit was ruled out by the War Production Board "for the duration," because of the wasteful amount of fabric it required. Truth to tell, no one cared.

Liquid stockings: In the summer months, during the war, we applied a foundation liquid to our legs, a product manufactured by all the big cosmetics firms which was supposed to create the look of hosiery on the legs. Then we performed the most impossible of feats. We drew a line up the back of the leg with an eyebrow pencil, simulating a seam. Oh, how horrible our legs looked when we came home from a date, all smudged and smeared from having danced and perspired and rubbed the backs of our knees against the chairs!

Rhyme-talk: A fad in 1947 was to talk in rhyme. That made you a real "solid-sender." The girl might ask her fellow, "What's cookin,' good lookin'?" to which he might reply, "Got no story, Mornin' Glory." Today, this might be called "rap."

Telephone booth antics: At St. Mary's College, twenty-two students crammed into a phone booth. This silly fad was going on all over the country. Every group was trying to break the record, which was thirty-four, according to *Life* magazine.

Flagpole watching: Like the flagpole sitters of the twenties, new flagpole daredevils emerged in 1946, and crowds gathered to watch them. The fad reached new heights when one couple got married atop a flagpole in Ohio.

Pinups: What would our servicemen have done without their pinup girls inside their lockers? Most men had pictures of their wives or girlfriends in their wallets, but bigger and more visible by far were their posters of Betty Grable and Rita Hayworth, the most popular of the pinups. In Betty's most famous poster, she's seen from the back, looking over her shoulder, wearing a backless one-piece swimsuit with hands on her hips, her million-dollar legs the focus of the picture.

Rita's famous pose was a side view, taken as she was kneeling on her bed. Her head was turned toward the camera so that her hair fell over her shoulder, and she pursed her lips provocatively. She was wearing a gown with a black lace bodice and a white satin skirt, which showcased her generous endowments.

Some servicemen preferred Varga girl prints, sketched by the famous artist Varga. These were of girls scantily clad and deliciously curvaceous. Their trademark: their long voluptuous legs.

Arthur Murray: A fad of the late forties was ballroom dancing, taught in the Arthur Murray Studios all over America. "Thrill your partner," the ad said. "Become a good dancer in just a few hours. Learn the waltz, the fox trot, the rhumba, and the tango." In New Orleans, the Arthur Murray Studio was in the Roosevelt Hotel (now the Fairmont).

Pyramid Clubs: When I was working at the telephone company in 1948, one of the other service representatives came to work one day with a story about a get-rich-quick scheme called the Pyramid Club. All I would have to do, she said, was send a dollar to the person at the top of the list of ten people she gave me, then remove his name from the list and add my own name to the bottom. Then I'd have to send a letter to ten friends of my own telling them that if they did the same, they would receive $10,000 within thirty days. After that, I could just sit back and wait for the money to roll in. It sounded good to me. I sent my dollar off without delay. Laboriously, I wrote my letters and dropped them in the mailbox.

At supper that night, I told Al and my parents about it. Al had seen something about it in *Life* magazine, a picture of a woman holding up two handfuls of money, about two thousand dollars worth, that she had received in a Pyramid Club.

My father said, "Well, theoretically it's possible, of course, but this isn't new, you know. I've seen this around before, and these clubs always collapse because the people you send the letters to can't all find ten more people to send them to. It's almost a mathematical impossibility. Besides, a lot of them don't want to be bothered."

"So?" I asked.

"So just suppose it all works perfectly for you. That means you've used up 10,000 people in your pyramid alone. What are all the other pyramid clubs in New Orleans going to do?"

"Who cares?" I asked. "Too bad about them."

Al and my father laughed. But I'd get the last laugh. I knew I was going to be rich. I waited patiently and at the end of the month, I got back one dollar. It was some consolation that there was at least one other person in the city as foolish as I was.

Moron's Ecstacy: This was just *one* of the names for the crazy concoctions made of ice cream in 1946. The treats included fruit, ice cream, whipped cream, syrup, nuts, and sprinkles, or any combination thereof. Americans had been deprived of sugar-based treats during the war and wanted to make up for it. They gobbled down 714 million gallons of ice cream the first year after the war.

Canasta: In 1949, an Argentine card game was sweeping the country. It was called *Canasta*. The U.S. Playing Card Company received 600,000 requests for rule books in a single month.

Crazy advertising: "Madman" Muntz of used-car fame "wanted to give cars away but his wife wouldn't let him." He was the postwar king of used-car sales, advertising this way on billboards and radio. Arthur Godfrey's folksey chatter earned him big money as a radio and TV announcer, plugging products he made you believe he really liked.

Henry Morgan was a radio and TV announcer who broke ground by razzing the products he advertised. He alienated some sponsors, but he got a lot of people talking about the products. On TV, he wore earmuffs so he wouldn't have to hear the breakfast cereal he was eating as it snapped and crackled.

Singing commercials were a craze, like "Chiquita Banana" and "Pepsi Cola Hits the Spot."

Beauty marks: Little adhesive patches made of black silk cut in the shapes of crescent moons, stars, cats, and crosses were applied to the face to accentuate the eye or the lips. The fad was brief but it was just one more example of America's craving for fantasy.

Tulane Stadium, October 1947.

CHAPTER SIXTEEN

Sports in the Forties

New Orleans is a sports-loving town, always has been. This was especially true during World War II, when recreation of any kind was badly needed as a distraction from fear and loneliness. And the forties, strange as it seems, produced some of the best athletes the city has ever seen.

HIGH SCHOOL FOOTBALL CHAMPIONS

Prep football in the thirties and forties was as important to New Orleans sports lovers as college football. And of course there was no talk yet of a professional team for the city. High school games drew enormous crowds, and fans were rabid in their devotion to their chosen schools.

The high schools that won city and state championships most often in the forties were Jesuit and Holy Cross, with Easton and Fortier winning one title each. Those were the glory days for Jesuit and Holy Cross. Jesuit started out the decade with city and state championship teams in 1940 and 1941. They came back as champions in 1943, and in 1946 they swept the boards clean with city and state Championships in football, basketball, baseball, and track, as well as the World Championship in American Legion Baseball. They were terrors in all arenas.

In 1940, the outstanding football players at Jesuit were O. J. Key, Tony diBartolo, Leonard Finley (later a quarterback at Tulane), and Paul Limont (later an end for Notre Dame). In 1941, diBartolo returned with Wally Schmidt, Jerry Ford (now of Ford Models, Inc. in New York), Lucien Caruso, and Al Widmer. In 1943, the Blue Jay stars were Ray Coates and Norman Hodgins. In 1946, the year of all-champs, the big guns were John Petitbon and Pat Rooney, football; Hugh Oser, who played all four sports; and Monroe ("Money") Caballero, who played football, basketball, and baseball.

Holy Cross won its first city championship of the decade against Nicholls High in 1944 in the CYO Bowl, boasting such stars as Joe Ernst, Hillary Chollet, and

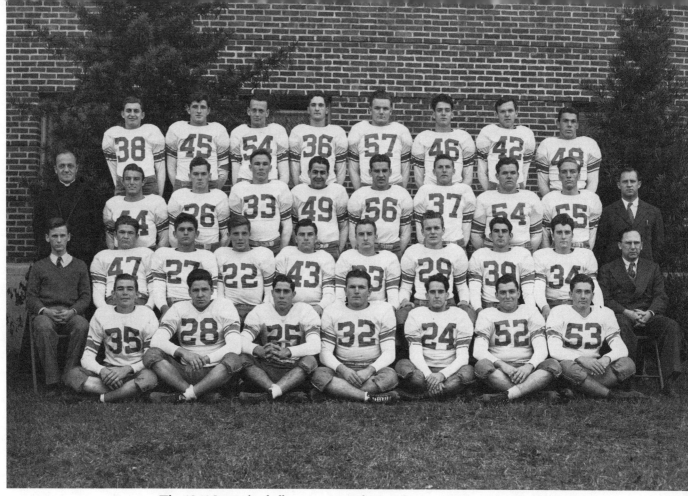

The 1941 Jesuit football team, city and state champs. Author's husband is in front row, third from left.

Ted Mace. In 1945, Ernst led his team to the state championship. In 1947, Holy Cross beat Easton to the championship, without Easton's stalwart Les Kennedy, who was unable to play. Holy Cross returned in 1949 to win again, with stars Joe Heap and Butsy Zimmerman.

Easton's one championship came against Jesuit in 1942, when Ray Prats, Eddie Price (later All-American at Tulane; still later, with the New York Giants), Jerry Comeaux, and Warren Thomas led their team to victory. Fortier could thank Ridley Boudreaux for its one city championship in 1948.

In this decade the best high school teams in the state came from New Orleans.

COLLEGE FOOTBALL IN NEW ORLEANS

The rivalry between the Tulane Green Wave and the LSU Tigers was hot throughout the decade. Tulane lost to Texas A&M, Southwestern Conference champs, 14–13 in the first Sugar Bowl game of the decade. Fans crowded the Tulane stadium to witness the talents of Bobby ("Jitterbug") Kellogg (All-Southeastern halfback), Fred Cassibry (later Judge Cassibry), Harley McCollum, and Carl Dailey.

The Greenies also played Notre Dame several times in the forties, losing badly. But then Notre Dame held the national championship in 1946, 1947, and 1949. In 1949, the Tulane Greenies, with Eddie Price and company, were the SEC champions in spite of the fact that they were defeated by the LSU Tigers by a score of 21–0 and by Notre Dame by the unbelievable score of 46–7. Tulane was not invited to a Bowl game that year.

From 1926 on, all major sporting events were held in the Tulane Stadium, which was eventually expanded into an 81,000 seat arena on Tulane's campus. It was the home of the Green Wave but it was also the Sugar Bowl's home from 1935 to 1974.

LOYOLA BASKETBALL

During the war years, Loyola chalked up three highly successful basketball seasons, one climaxed by a national championship. Coach Jack Orsley took his team to Kansas City and returned home with the title. The Men of the South were pitted against the Illinois Normal Maroons, and the lead changed constantly. Johnny Casteix's "money shot" from the side court sent the Wolfpack into the championship. Then the Wolfpack soundly defeated the Pepperdine Waves of Los Angeles by a 49–36 score. This brought Loyola her first National Basketball Championship.

The team's record for the season was 25 wins, 5 defeats. Leroy Chollet was named to the All-American squad for his outstanding play in the tournament. "Red" Hultberg gained the second team.

When Loyola won the National Intercollegiate Tournament in 1945, Leroy Chollet and "Red" Hultberg were named All-American.

Close play at first.

VARSITY BASEBALL RETURNS TO LOYOLA

In the spring of 1946, a group of aspiring players answered Coach Orsley's call for the first Loyola baseball team since 1928. Among them were Bob Gibbens, Dave Brennan, Russ Cresson, "Beanie" Shirer, Weldon Cousins, Jack Eumont, and Bill Treuting, who worked together for an impressive 8–2 record.

In the spring of 1947, the Wolfpack was victorious in 13 of 19 games, playing against teams like Mississippi College and Northern Illinois. As a team, the hitting was exceptional, as the .279 average will attest. The hard-hitting out-fielder, Charlie Glueck, was leading the club with a neat .421 when he slid into home and fractured his ankle, putting him out for the rest of the season.

Sparked by diminutive Don Wetzel, the Pack's fielding was far above average. Other outstanding players were Gus Riordan, Tommy Wedig, Jack ("Errol") Flynn, Norman Hodgins, Whitey Jackson, Al Weidmann, Pete Tusa, and Jack McNulty.

BASEBALL—NEW ORLEANS' OWN PELICANS

When the Pelicans opened the 1940 season, it had been only five years since their last Southern Association title, which was followed by a Dixie Series Championship over Galveston. They played throughout the forties, although young players were called into the military and older men filled in as best they could till the pros came back from the war.

In 1947, New Orleans enjoyed its finest season in postwar history. The club won 93 games and lost 59. They almost won the pennant, but had to bow to the Bears of Mobile, who finished on top by a mere half-game. The lineup was formidable: Al Flair, George Stumpf, Mel Rue, Pete Modica, Red Lavigne, and Jesse Danna. The team attracted an all-time Pelican record attendance of 400,036 fans to old Pelican Stadium.

Al Flair was the club's outstanding player. He batted .308 and led the Southern Association in home runs (24) and runs batted in (128). Fans at the August 29, 1947 contest will never forget a home run off the bat of Al Flair, a drive which sailed some 420 feet over the center-field fence, one of the longest ever hit at the old ball park.

From 1915 to 1938, the ball park at the corner of Tulane and South Carrollton was called Heinemann Park. After 1938, it was called Pelican Stadium, home of the New Orleans Pelicans till 1957, when it was torn down to make way for the Fountainbleau Motor Hotel. The Pelicans, a team which entered professional baseball in 1887, lost their franchise in 1960.

Another baseball team worthy of mention in the forties was the 1946 Jesuit-based World Champion American Legion team which included a pitcher who was Mayor-to-be Moon Landrieu.

Al Flair, the Pelicans' first baseman, hit one of the longest home runs ever seen at Pelican Stadium on August 29, 1947. (Courtesy Arthur Schott)

Pelican Stadium, on Carrollton and Tulane, was home to the Pelican baseball team through the forties.

The Jax Girls. Front row: Dot Leckner, outfield; Selma Miencke, outfield; Evelyn Case, outfield; Dottie Pitts, catcher; Hazel Gill, second base; Skipper Daul, infielder. Back row: Frieda Savona, shortstop; Mary Pembo, first base; Olympia Savona, pitcher-infielder; Lottie Jackson, pitcher; Nina Korgan, pitcher; Dottie Walker, third base; Buck Brehn, coach. Not pictured: Blanche Soniat, Hazel Mermelliod, and manager Herd Ragas. (Courtesy Hazel Gill)

THE JAX GIRLS

In the 1940s, New Orleans had a nationally known women's team called the Jax Girls. At first they had been the Falstaff Girls, but their franchise was purchased by the Jackson Brewery. They hired players who defeated them to come and work at the Jackson Brewery so that they could play on the Jax Girls' team.

One such player was an outstanding shortstop called Frieda Savona, whose younger sister Olympia stayed with the team until the brewery closed. When Lottie Jackson was defeated in the finals of a national women's championship by Nina Korgan, pitcher, they hired Nina to play with the Jax Girls. Some outstanding local girls were Blanche Soniat, first baseman; Lillian Theard, left fielder; Mary Pembo, reserve first baseman; and Hazel Gill, second baseman. The Jax Girls won five national women's championships in a row starting in 1942.

PUTSY CABALLERO,
A MINOR IN A MAJOR LEAGUE

Ralph "Putsy" Caballero, the Philadelphia "Whiz Kid," played third base for the Phillies at age sixteen in September 1944. The week before, he'd been playing for Jesuit's American Legion team when Philadelphia scout Ed McGraw signed him for $8,000. Gernon Brown, his coach at Jesuit, told him to take the offer, and he was off to Philadelphia.

"I was playing legion ball one week," says Caballero, "and the next, I was in the Major Leagues. It was incredible."

Ralph ("Putsy") Caballero was sixteen when he first stepped up to the plate for the Philadelphia Phillies. (Courtesy Ralph Caballero)

Putsy was part of a Philadelphia youth movement, brought on by the fact that the Phillies had not won a pennant since 1915.

"They brought me and the other rookies up the last few weeks of the season," says Putsy, "and the fans yelled for the young guys to play. So Manager Freddie Fitzsimmons played me at third. I still hold the record for being the youngest player to play third in the majors."

Philadelphia sent Caballero to its minor league club in Utica, New York, for three years of seasoning. By 1948, he was a regular in the Phillies lineup. The highlight of his major career came in 1950, when the Phillies won the pennant and played Casey Stengel's Yankees in the World Series. The "Whiz Kids," so labeled because there were so many young men on the team, beat a vintage Dodgers team in Brooklyn on the final day of the pennant race. "The Dodgers had Gil Hodges, Jackie Robinson, Pee Wee Reese, and Roy Campanella," says Caballero.

Today Putsy finds baseball cards with his picture on them in his mail. He autographs them and mails them back to the owners. "They come to me from all over the country," he says. "I've been asked to go to Philadelphia for a baseball card show," he adds. "I'll probably do that some day."

BOXING, A NEW ORLEANS FAVORITE

Chester Banta, winner of the Southern AAU Championship for four years and later a trainer in the forties, worked with young fighters at his Knights of Columbus gym at 836 Carondelet. He knows a lot about fighters, promoters, and gyms of the period.

"Harry Greb, middleweight champion of the world, came to New Orleans to fight in the old Coliseum Arena," says Banta. "Two promoters, Heard Ragas and 'Leapin' Lou Messina, promoted fighters who worked out at Curley's Gym on the corner of St. Charles and Poydras.

"A very colorful matchmaker in New Orleans in the late forties was Lou Raymond. There was an area just outside the Times-Picayune building called 'Raymond's Beach,' where he made matches with the fight gang. He lived in a hotel just across from Curley's Gym on St. Charles."

Two of the gyms where fighters worked out in those days were Marty Burke's Gym at 229 Bourbon across from Gluck's Restaurant; and Robinson's Gym at 139 Baronne, next door to the Roosevelt Hotel (now the Fairmont). Fred McFarlane was a boxing director for the New Orleans Athletic Club, a good place to work out in the early 1940s.

Almost every neighborhood had boxing clubs. In the 1940s, the Ducassan brothers, Maxie and Bernard, were well-known fighters in New Orleans. Bernard Ducassan won the national middleweight championship in Boston when he was fourteen years old. He fought Sugar Ray Robinson in 1948, but this was one year too soon. Some believe that in one year more, he would have beaten Robinson.

Some of the best amateur fighters of the period were Francis Kercheval, who turned professional in 1939; and the Shaw twins, Harry and Bob. Harry, 147 pounds, was a welterweight; Bob, 155 pounds, was a middleweight.

The fight game was segregated in New Orleans until the sixties.

Tulane Avenue looking toward the river. Top right, St. Joseph's Church; top left, cupola of Dixie Brewery; halfway down to right (long building on Jeff Davis Parkway), Dibert Bancroft (now gone); upper right, Falstaff Brewery.

CHAPTER SEVENTEEN

Closing the Half-Century

AT THE END OF the half-century, New Orleans was still just a glorified country town. Thousands of young New Orleanians had been sent to the other side of the world and had suffered through a devastating war, but they'd returned to find things just about the same way they'd left them, and for good reason. There had been a wartime moratorium on civilian construction, due to a shortage of materials and labor, so the streets were badly in need of repairs and many buildings were deteriorating. The things that *were* different had been caused by the return of the veterans: the housing shortage, the job shortage, the mad rush to the colleges by veterans wanting to use their G.I. Bills, and the epidemic of weddings.

G.I. BILL DEGREES

In 1949, my husband Al graduated from Loyola on the G.I. Bill, completing his college requirements like thousands of other veterans that year. He received a bachelor of business administration. It was the first year the university had awarded this degree. Heretofore, it had been a bachelor of science in business administration. Now "business" had come into its own, and needed its own separate college.

For the past three years (colleges still ran the accelerated program), he'd been going to school, studying, and working part time at Maison Blanche.

College, as the returning G.I.s discovered, was not the carefree time of the prewar years. To these men, several years older than the high school grads they went to class with, it was serious business. They *had* to study hard and graduate. Their employment as married men depended on it. They participated in some fraternity parties and student dances, and they enjoyed school sports, both intramural and varsity, but their studies came first. Many of the veterans had children by the time they graduated.

After college, Al sent out many resumés but remained unemployed for three months. There were ten good men available for every job, and most of them had business degrees. For the first time in our country's history, college degrees were a dime a dozen.

I'LL TAKE ANY JOB YOU'VE GOT

At last Al took a job with Consolidated Companies, a wholesale food distributing company that handled Autocrat canned products. His territory was in the Evangeline country around Lafayette, where he called on small grocery stores and took orders. This kept him out of New Orleans for five days a week and home only on weekends. For this he earned $220 a month which, even in those days, was not a good salary for a male college graduate. But it was work. That was the best thing you could say about it.

I was very unhappy about his job. Fortunately for me, we were still living with my parents, and I was working, so I had lots of company, but to see him only two days a week depressed me terribly. In the years to come, he would have several other jobs before he found the work which became his lifetime career—selling radio advertising and eventually managing the sales department of a radio station, which he did till he retired.

In 1949, I was still at the Telephone Company on Baronne Street, but I was a coach. I trained service reps to do the work I'd done for two years, handling customer requests and complaints. It was wonderful work, teaching enthusiastic adults rather than unruly children.

NEIGHBORHOOD MERCHANTS

At the close of the decade, neighborhoods still had corner groceries and drugstores, but changes were to come in the fifties. In August 1946, John G. Schwegmann, Jr., and his cousins and Wilfred Meyer founded Schwegmann Brothers Giant Super Market when they opened the 40,000-square-foot St. Claude Street store. It was the first grocery-market in New Orleans to obtain a license to sell fresh meat. In 1950, the huge 90,000-square-foot Airline Highway store was completed, a phenomenon in the industry. It was the first of dozens of supermarkets in the city that would eventually close down the little independent grocer.

This huge Schwegmann's opened on Airline Highway in 1950; the first one was on St. Claude Avenue. (Courtesy Schwegmann Brothers)

Breaux's Grocery, 3600 Cleveland Avenue, was a typical neighborhood store (1946).

L&L food store, 7826 Sycamore, also served area homemakers (June 1946).

Mr. Herbert still operated his one-man butcher shop on St. Peter Street, and my Memere still shopped there, though not every day as she had in the thirties. We had an electric refrigerator now with a meat keeper, and meat could be stored for several days without spoiling. But she still made Mr. Herbert hold up the slices of meat so she could scrutinize them for quality and freshness before making a decision.

Vendors still came by almost every day, still in wagons pulled by straw-hatted mules.

WEREN'T YOU RELATED TO . . .

When shopping as a young married woman with my mother and grandmother in K&B or the H. G. Hill Store, I was often amused by their conversations with people they met and recognized. "Aren't you one of the LaRoccas?" Mother would ask. "Didn't your family live on Dauphine Street back around 1915?"

If the answer was yes, all kinds of questions followed. "Didn't your brother move to Mid-City sometime in the twenties? I thought so. We useta see him in church with his wife, remember, Mama? St. Anthony's, sure." And then they'd discuss all the aunts and uncles they remembered, and ask questions about their children.

Everybody knew everybody. They still do. I thought it was funny then, but now I do the same thing myself. I always say that if you live fifty years in New Orleans, you know everybody, one way or another.

View of the city from New Orleans Public Service gas holder. (Courtesy Louisiana Power & Light)

DISEASES AND REMEDIES

People worried a lot about polio in the forties. An epidemic of the disease in 1946 killed or crippled hundreds. The Salk vaccine would not come along until the fifties. The papers warned that the disease might be transmitted in swimming pools, but Audubon and City Park pools were still crowded every day in the summer months.

Antibiotics had been welcomed as a miracle of modern medicine for serious infections, but for minor ailments, many still relied on the old-time preventatives: Milk of Magnesia every weekend whether you needed it or not, cream of tartar in summertime to cool the blood, and cooling down after strenuous exercise before drinking a glass of cold water.

WEEKENDS AND VACATIONS

My family still spent time in Waveland in the summer months. My father's aunt had a home there, and in the late forties, my father's sister built one of her own in the piney woods near the railroad depot. Al and I spent weekends there in the summer when we had free time.

A few times, we went with Bob and Vernon by train to the Gulf Coast and spent a weekend at the White House in Biloxi, where we swam and loafed and played bridge and ate seafood.

On two different occasions at the end of the forties, several of my friends from Loyola and their husbands (a few now with toddlers) rented a camp at Little Woods, brought cooked food, and spent the weekend talking, tanning, and playing bridge. The men always recall a night when they cooked, making meatballs and spaghetti, with gravy they still claim was 90 percent beer.

The Edgewater Gulf Hotel, between Gulfport and Biloxi, was a wonderful retreat for young couples and their children, and we went there for ten years with our "couple" friends. The children could play on the beach or out on the huge front lawns without fear of traffic, while the mothers sat in lawn chairs beneath the oaks and read novels. We loved the drugstore with its chocolate sodas and club sandwiches, its first-aid supplies, and its gifts for someone having a birthday.

Pontchartrain Beach in the forties was a cool, fun place to go in the summer. Although it was surrounded by military installations during the war, or perhaps *because* it was, it thrived during those years. It flourished on the patronage of servicemen stationed in the immediate area who needed fun and distractions in that time of tension.

On Labor Day in 1945, just two weeks after the war ended (but before our sweethearts came home), several girlfriends and I went to spend the day at the Beach and have a picnic. An ad in the paper spoke of "cool picnic shelters and the spectacular Starlight Revue, with the Selts performing high-perch balancing and Le Volos, a tight-wire thrill."

Muriel, Sue, Mary Joyce, Nellie, Vernon, and I went out there to eat a picnic lunch and enjoy the rides and the free show. I remember that we wore playsuits, shorts with matching skirts, so that we could ride the bus to the Beach modestly dressed. It rained in torrents that day, but we found shelter under the bathhouse, and came out when the weather cleared. All in all, it was a wonderful day.

From 1946 on, Al and I attended many LSU games played in Baton Rouge. We drove there with several other couples, had dinner in some little restaurant

Edgewater Gulf Hotel between Gulfport and Biloxi, where young couples spent weekends or vacations in the late forties.

Audubon Park Zoo in the forties. A cupola tops the elephant house. The zoo was a fun weekend attraction.

Audubon Park aviary.

on arriving, and then walked to the game, in the midst of screaming co-eds and musicians clanging cymbals and beating drums. What spirit we found there, in the "Ole War Skule!" And did we dress up for those games—in dressy suits and silk blouses, nylon stockings and high-heeled shoes! The men wore suits, dress shirts, and ties.

When we didn't make the trip to Baton Rouge, we usually saw the Tulane Greenies on Saturdays. I worked half-days on Saturdays at the Telephone Company, and Al came to meet me there. We took the streetcar to the Sugar Bowl Stadium on the Tulane campus, hopefully to watch the Green Wave roll over its opponent, unless that opponent was the Tigers of Baton Rouge.

Author and husband gather with friends for a Tiger football game in Baton Rouge (late 1940s).

SCREEN AND STAGE

In May of 1946, *The Zeigfeld Follies* was playing at the Loew's State Theater, starring William Powell and Louise Rainer. The Movie of the Year was *The Best Years of Our Lives,* with Fredric March, Myrna Loy, Dana Andrews, and Teresa Wright. Reflecting the aftermath of the war, it told the story of veterans returning home to find a housing shortage, a job shortage, and the stark reality of life in the real world for a paraplegic war hero. Harold Russell, a former paratrooper whose hands had been blown off on D-Day, played the part of the disabled veteran and won an Academy Award for his supporting role.

We enjoyed a treasure trove of musicals in the forties, with Betty Grable and Dan Dailey, Alice Faye and John Payne, Fred Astaire and Ginger Rogers, Eleanor Powell, Vera Ellen, Ann Miller, Danny Kaye, and dozens of others. Musicals were almost all in color in the late forties, the brightness of the colors accentuating the cheerfulness of the song-and-dance routines. We saw most of our movies at the neighborhood shows, the Carrollton or the Imperial. A trip to town for a movie was usually a Saturday night dress-up affair.

Three movies remain my favorites from the forties, and since they are still shown today, I can't help but think that my choices were good ones. One was *Yankee Doodle Dandy,* which Al and I saw together on a Tuesday afternoon in the summer of '42 at the Orpheum. I had only morning classes that summer, and he took a two-hour lunch break from his stockroom job at Maison Blanche. We bought a couple of hamburgers, "with everything," at the one-and-only Lee's Hamburger Stand next door to the Orpheum, and hid the bag as we went inside the theater. Then, in the balcony, we enjoyed our delicious sandwiches as we watched what we considered a fabulous movie. It still plays every Fourth of July, so apparently, others shared our sentiments.

My second favorite was *It's a Wonderful Life,* with James Stewart and Donna Reed, and I don't have to tell anyone how many Christmases that classic has been repeated.

The third was *Holiday Inn,* with Fred Astaire, Bing Crosby, and beautiful Marjorie Reynolds, who would later have a lead in a long-running TV sitcom, "The Life of Riley." Al and I saw this one together on a Sunday afternoon at the old Gentilly Theater shortly before he went into the service. It played once again for Christmas recently.

Annie Get Your Gun, with a young Ethel Merman, was touted the best play on Broadway in the middle forties. But *Oklahoma* by Rodgers and Hammerstein, with the fantastic choreography of Agnes deMille, had revolutionized Broadway musicals, setting a format for dozens of others to come. Songs from that play were still on the jukeboxes in the late forties, songs like "People Will Say We're in Love."

In 1947, Marlon Brando made his stage debut in Tennessee Williams' *A Streetcar Named Desire*, as the crude Stanley Kowalski to Jessica Tandy's pseudo-aristocratic Blanche DuBois. *Streetcar* had been written by Tennessee Williams when he was living in the French Quarter in New Orleans between 1940 and 1947. A wanderer, Williams said, "If I can be said to have a home, it is New Orleans." *Streetcar*, set in New Orleans, established him as one of the nation's leading playwrights.

DANCE BANDS

Occasionally we went to the Blue Room, when there was a band or a singer we particularly liked, and if we'd saved enough money. A Sunday afternoon matinee was cheaper than a night performance, so we availed ourselves of that. And oh, how we loved the big band sound we heard in that famous nightclub. It gave us goose bumps all over. The bands who came there were not Jimmy and Tommy Dorsey, Harry James, or Artie Shaw, but successful bands on a slightly lower rung of the ladder, like Louis Prima's band. We did not know it, but the Big Band era was closing with the decade, and a totally different style of pop music was waiting in the wings.

Easter Sunday 1946, dressed for the Blue Room matinee. Note the footbridge over the Orleans Canal, which was not yet filled in.

Pat Barberot's Orchestra at Jim's Plaza Club, summer of 1948. Saxophones: Joseph ("Chops") Lambert, David Daigle, John Favalora, Bill Henneberg, Pat Barberot. Piano, Joe Salvagio; bass, Rupert Surcouf; drums, Johnny Lais. Trumpets: Sidney Prendergast, Mickey Harris, Al Montalto. Trombones: Eddie Schmidt, Herbie Boasso. Vocalist, Kris Karen. (Courtesy Rupert Surcouf)

There were many bands of young musicians that started in the forties in New Orleans, before and after the war. Although some were made up almost entirely of teenagers, they were outstanding for their talent. They quickly gained popularity and were in demand for proms and dances and Saturday night spots, where teenagers went to dance. Pat Barberot's band played at proms and dances, and found its first regular spot at the Plaza Club in Kenner in 1947 and 1948. Larry Veca's band played at the Terrace Club on Downman Road in the early forties.

"In 1946, Al Belleto put together a sixteen-piece band with players like Sam Butera," said Rupert Surcouf, bass player, who provided most of this information. "I was in that band. With the help of WDSU and the announcer Gay Batson, we entered a national teenage band contest sponsored by *Look* magazine. The band won the Southern division and then we went to Carnegie Hall for the Nationals. We did not win, but Sam Butera was picked the outstanding teenage musician and his picture was on the cover of *Look* magazine. Al Belleto later played at a club on the Airline Highway called Al's Club, with a band called The Moods."

Surcouf adds, "I've been playing since I was fifteen. I was big for my age, but sometimes I still got put out for being too young to be in a nightclub. We got paid six-seven-six on weekends at the Terrace Club. Six dollars, that is. The Saturday night gig was seven, because it was longer. And when we played for Pat Barberot at the Plaza in Kenner, we got an extra dollar a night for traveling money, since the club was 'out of town.'"

Al Belleto's Band, winners of the Southern division of the national teenage band contest sponsored by Look *magazine, 1946. First row: Mike Carubba, Ronald St. Germain, David Daigle, Sam Butera, Emile Mancuso, Al Belleto. Second row: Jack Delanie, Larry Valentino, Bill Langenstein, Mickey Harris, Buddy Bishop, George Peterson. Drums, C. D. McKnight; bass, Rupert Surcouf; piano, Eddie Fenasci; not pictured on trumpet, Benny Clement. (Courtesy Rupert Surcouf)*

The Larry Veca Band at the Terrace Club on Downman Road, 1945. Front row: Rupert Surcouf, Louis Wise, Rudolph Valentino, Johnny Veca, and Larry Veca. Second row: Louis Prector, Pat Easterling, Ducky Gray, Larry Valentino. Piano: Lawrence Veca. (Courtesy Rupert Surcouf)

"Joe Kluchin followed us when we left the Plaza Club. His band was called The Southerners. Some players who were with him then are still playing around town today.

"The first band I played with was Johnny Vega's Band at the Cotton Club. He had all good musicians, many of whom later started their own bands.

"Larry Veca also had a first class band. They had fine arrangements. Many players with Veca later played with Russ Papalia, Johnny Vega, Johnny Detroit, and Rupert Copponex.

"During World War II, a twenty-piece navy band came to New Orleans, and stayed here after the war, playing on Bourbon Street. Almost every night spot had a band."

Another popular group of the forties was Russ Papalia's Band. Besides their regular gigs, they played for USO dances during the war to entertain the soldiers. Another entertainer in demand was Tony Almerico, whose band played for soldiers at Lagarde Hospital on the lakefront and at the USO centers. In his career, he played on the steamer *President* and the *Capitol,* and in the late forties, at the Parisian Room on Royal Street.

Pete Fountain, in the forties, played with the Dukes of Dixieland and the Basin Street Six. He was playing music until three in the morning and then going to Warren Easton High School all day, and falling asleep in his classes. Pete told this story when he was on the "Angela" show on TV. His teacher asked him why he kept falling asleep, and Pete told him about his music gigs. "How much do you make?" the teacher asked. "One hundred fifty dollars a week," Pete said. "Then why don't you quit school and concentrate on your music?" the teacher asked. And that's what Pete Fountain did. Pete's first break came when he was invited to play with the Lawrence Welk band.

Al Hirt, New Orleans' master trumpeter, had a classical background for music. He didn't play jazz until after the war. At Jesuit and Fortier high schools, his talents were rewarded. Vincent Liberto, manager at Masson's Restaurant for many years, tells the story that since Al always won the trophy for Best Musician at Jesuit, he, Vincent, always came in second. For that reason, Vincent now donates The Vincent J. Liberto Award for Instrumental Music to the *Second* Best Musician at Jesuit High School.

Al Hirt's first big-time away-from-home job was with the George White Scandals. Later, he played for the lady bandleader Ina Ray Hutton. But his big break came when he competed in the Horace Heidt Contest at the Municipal Auditorium. He not only won but went touring the country with the Horace Heidt band.

After that he started playing in New Orleans. He played with the Dawnbusters on WWL early morning radio. He played for Carnival balls. Then he started his own band, which played at the Preview Lounge. That was where he was seen by Monique Van Vooren, who was starring at the Blue Room at the time. She called her husband, a booking agent, and told him to fly to New Orleans. She had someone she wanted him to hear. After he heard Al, he booked him on the "Dinah Shore Show" and Al's career took off.

Other New Orleans musicians worthy of note were Peter Toma, an accordion player, who was at the Fountain Lounge in the Roosevelt, and Leon Kelner, who also played the Fountain Lounge.

Surcouf says, "Three well-known bandleaders played the Carnival balls almost exclusively in the forties: Rene Louapre, a trumpeter, whose band played for Rex and Momus—he had first-class musicians, who could play anything from the opera *Aida* to jazz; Russ Papalia, a trombone player; and Johnny Detroit, a trumpeter. That was the criteria. If your band played for the balls, you had a class outfit.

"One other band is worthy of mention for the period of the forties. Lloyd Alexander [real name: Irwin Knight] played the trumpet and had a big band, a quality band. He did spot work, took bookings. He usually had a singer."

The Basin Street Six played every night at Lenfant's in the late forties. Here they're on the Brown's Velvet TV show. Left to right: Roy Zimmerman (piano), Joe Rotis, George Girard, Pete Fountain, Bunny Franks (bass), Charlie Duke (drums). (Courtesy Pete and Beverly Fountain)

BOOKS

The best-selling novels of 1945 and 1946 were *Forever Amber* and *The Robe*, which said something for the eclectic tastes of modern readers. Other favorites were *Green Dolphin Street*, *Leave Her to Heaven*, *The Black Rose*, *Fountainhead*, and *The King's General*.

Other best sellers of the forties were *River Road* and *Dinner at Antoine's* by New Orleans' beloved Frances Parkenson Keyes. She found the New Orleans setting immensely saleable, and used it again and again. She wrote fifty-one novels, most of which made the best-seller list, and although she did not win great critical acclaim, she won mine, and she sold a lot of books. I adored her writing.

SEGREGATION IN NEW ORLEANS

In schools and restaurants, public transit and public bathrooms, segregation was still the law. Blacks still sat behind the signs in streetcars and drank from the water fountains marked "Colored." The "Colored" shopping area of town was on South Rampart Street, between Canal and Howard Avenue. You rarely saw a black person in the main Canal Street stores, and if you did, you also saw white shoppers making a wide path for her, their eyes following her like daggers.

During the war, troops had been segregated. My husband told me that. There were no "colored" men in his unit, but all that was to change under Truman.

Gentilly Public Library, 3001 Gentilly Boulevard, served many of the city's book lovers (1949).

Southern Railway Station sheds on Basin Street, terminating on Canal Street in the forties.

TRANSPORTATION

In the forties, the only bridge that crossed the Mississippi in the vicinity of New Orleans was the Huey P. Long Bridge. The Greater New Orleans Mississippi River Bridge (now the Crescent City Connection) would not be completed until 1958. Ferries at the foot of Canal Street were the only means of transportation for commuters from Algiers.

The Southern Railway Station was at Canal and Basin Street. That was the one you took to go to New York. The L&N Railroad left from Canal Street at the river for cities along the Gulf Coast. We took that train to go to Gulfport on our honeymoon. The Old Union Station was where the Union Passenger Terminal and bus depot are today, at Rampart and Julia streets. Al's train left from there when he departed for boot camp in California.

Under Mayor Morrison, plans were underway to combine all these railroad lines into one terminal, thus eliminating the traffic tie-ups at busy intersections in the heart of the city.

SITTING BEFORE THE DOOR

In spite of all these progressive developments, and in spite of the unusual living conditions during and after the war, people still sat outside after supper, swatting the air with their palmetto fans. Air-conditioning would not drive us all indoors until the late fifties and early sixties. There was little crime then, so the ladies could sit outdoors and chat, exchanging recipes and news of their families, and talking about the towels they'd bought on sale that day at Maison Blanche, while the children played "One, Two, Three, Red Light" and "Kick the Can" in the streets till they were called in at bedtime.

FUNERALS AND WAKES

Funerals were long, drawn-out affairs, and mourning was loud and unrestrained. Families still stayed upstairs in the funeral homes overnight, not allowing the "body" to be left alone its last night before burial. Children were still lifted up over the side of the coffin to kiss the dearly departed before the coffin was closed. And at the cemetery, we watched while the diggers shoveled dirt over the coffin. We were spared nothing.

Ladies still wore black to funerals and close relatives still dressed in mourning for a reasonable time. Visits to the cemeteries were compulsory in most families on All Saints' Day, Christmas, and the birthday of the deceased. People still whitewashed their graves, and kept the vases clean and the flowers fresh. Most elderly ladies like my Memere stopped going to the movies for life when someone close to them died.

FOOD

During the Depression and in the forties, there were small ma-and-pa family restaurants all over town, where you could get a meal of fried chicken, beans and rice, and turnip greens for a dollar or so. It was Southern food but it wasn't called "soul food" yet.

A more elegant variety of Creole food was served in the fancy Vieux Carré restaurants like Arnaud's, Galatoire's, Antoine's, and Broussard's. After the war,

Butter Krisp Restaurant at 2010 St. Charles Avenue.

The Camellia Grill, South Carrollton Avenue, a popular uptown eating spot even in the late 1940s.

Brennan's began to feature its famous egg dishes, making the restaurant a "must" as a breakfast stop on a visitor's itinerary. Antoine's fame had been built on its luscious oyster dishes like Oysters Rockefeller and Oysters Bienville. Galatoire's was the place to go for Shrimp Remoulade and cold crabmeat. And if you wanted sumptuous fish dishes, the restaurant was Arnaud's.

But Creole cooking remained popular with black and white people throughout the forties. The craving for red beans and rice, fried chicken, seafood gumbo, and stews cooked with a roux never diminished in New Orleanians. The ingredients for these staples were not rationed, hard to get, or expensive.

Rush hour, March 1946, on Carondelet Street near Canal Street.

NEW CARS! HOW LONG DO WE HAVE TO WAIT?

After the war, the first new cars to roll off the assembly line arrived in 1946. The sleek new Buicks, Fords, and Chevrolets that had been so long awaited were admired by all, for no new cars had been seen since 1942. The special four-door Buick sedan sold for $1,580. In the Super Estate Wagon, its redesigned fenders made it Buick's most changed model. The list price was $2,594. This was for the rich, we thought.

The Chevy was a less expensive car, starting at $1,072. This was more like it, but we couldn't even afford that yet. For running errands, we kept on using my father's old '36 Chevy.

MARDI GRAS

When Mardi Gras returned in 1946, after four years of absence during the war, the people of New Orleans were ready for it. Our group of couples, some not yet married, rode on a flatbed truck in the Krewe of Crescent City, a truck parade organized that year to follow the Rex Parade behind the Elks' Krewe of Orleanians, an older truck parade organized in 1930.

For the Mid-City Parade, I went to Audrey's house, as I had before the war. Audrey lived on Canal Street, on the parade route, and her family had had "open house" for that parade since they'd moved there in 1939. Mid-City was a favorite among the children. In 1947, it introduced animated floats. It attracted national attention with its "Greatest Bands in Dixie" Contest.

In 1941, the Krewe of Venus, the first female parade, took to the streets. Neon lights now decorated the floats, and in the forties, both the West Bank and St. Bernard parishes had their own Carnival activities for the first time. Flambeaux carriers still illuminated the parades and added flavor with their own style of strutting. And the decade ended with Louis Armstrong as the king of Zulu.

MUNICIPAL GOVERNMENT

After 1946, Mayor Chep Morrison was at the helm of city government, giving it an aura of honesty and integrity. He had broken the control of the Old Regular "Ring" politics in New Orleans and set the city on a whole new track. His accomplishments, in spite of unrelenting opposition by Governor Earl K. Long, were to carry the Crescent City proudly into the second half of the twentieth century.

Index